Nashville Midwives

The midwives of Music City!

Welcome to Nashville, Tennessee! The home of country music *and* Skylar, Brianna and Lori. Midwives at Legacy Women's Clinic, they dedicate their days and nights to their patients. But when Skylar, Brianna and Lori aren't helping to bring bundles of joy into the world, they are facing meet-cutes with colleagues that leave hearts racing! Will their love stories be so magical they could inspire the city's next big country star as they sing their latest hit on the Bluebird Café's stage...?

Find out in...

Skylar and Jared's story
Unbuttoning the Bachelor Doc

Brianna and Knox's story
The Rebel Doctor's Secret Child

Lori and Zach's story
Single Dad's Fake Fiancée

Available now!

Dear Reader,

While I'm sad to be leaving behind Nashville's Legacy Women's Clinic and the people that make it the city's premier obstetric clinic, I can't wait for you to get the chance to catch up with midwife Lori Mason and her friends. For the last few months Lori has seen her best friends, Sky and Bree, find their perfect match. Unfortunately, Lori hasn't been that lucky. Instead, she's gone through boyfriend after boyfriend, without one of them being *her* Mr. Right. That is, until she meets the new pediatrician in town, Dr. Zachary Morales. Talk about tall, dark and handsome—the man checks off all those boxes and more. There's only one problem. After the loss of his wife, he's not interested in any type of romance. His priority now is to provide a home for his son. And if that means faking an engagement, he knows that Lori, with all her romance-book knowledge, is perfect for the job. Maybe someone should have warned him how all those romance books ended. Or maybe he just needed to find out himself.

I hope you enjoy reading Lori and Zach's story as they discover that love has no limits.

Deanne

SINGLE DAD'S FAKE FIANCÉE

DEANNE ANDERS

MEDICAL ROMANCE

If you purchased this book without a cover you should be aware that this book is stolen property. It was reported as "unsold and destroyed" to the publisher, and neither the author nor the publisher has received any payment for this "stripped book."

ISBN-13: 978-1-335-94309-5

Single Dad's Fake Fiancée

Copyright © 2025 by Denise Chavers

All rights reserved. No part of this book may be used or reproduced in any manner whatsoever without written permission.

Without limiting the author's and publisher's exclusive rights, any unauthorized use of this publication to train generative artificial intelligence (AI) technologies is expressly prohibited.

This is a work of fiction. Names, characters, places and incidents are either the product of the author's imagination or are used fictitiously. Any resemblance to actual persons, living or dead, businesses, companies, events or locales is entirely coincidental.

For questions and comments about the quality of this book, please contact us at CustomerService@Harlequin.com.

TM and ® are trademarks of Harlequin Enterprises ULC.

 Harlequin Enterprises ULC
22 Adelaide St. West, 41st Floor
Toronto, Ontario M5H 4E3, Canada
www.Harlequin.com

Printed in U.S.A.

Deanne Anders was reading romance while her friends were still reading Nancy Drew, and she knew she'd hit the jackpot when she found a shelf of Harlequin Presents books in her local library. Years later she discovered the fun of writing her own. Deanne lives in Florida with her husband and their spoiled Pomeranian. During the day she works as a nursing supervisor. With her love of everything medical and romance, writing for Harlequin Medical Romance is a dream come true.

Books by Deanne Anders

Harlequin Medical Romance

The Surgeon's Baby Bombshell
Stolen Kiss with the Single Mom
Sarah and the Single Dad
The Neurosurgeon's Unexpected Family
December Reunion in Central Park
Florida Fling with the Single Dad
Pregnant with the Secret Prince's Babies
Flight Nurse's Florida Fairy Tale
A Surgeon's Christmas Baby

Nashville Midwives

Unbuttoning the Bachelor Doc
The Rebel Doctor's Secret Child

Visit the Author Profile page at Harlequin.com.

**Praise for
Deanne Anders**

"This story captivated me. I enjoyed every moment
[of] it. This is a great example of a medical romance.
Deanne Anders is an amazing writer!"
—*Goodreads* on *The Surgeon's Baby Bombshell*

CHAPTER ONE

PALE PINK ROSES and white baby's breath filled tall crystal vases while twinkling lights lit the large barn that had been transformed into a rustic fairyland. A string quartet played softly in the background as almost a hundred guests, all the happy couple's coworkers and family members, raised their glasses to toast the newly married couple. It was a picture-perfect moment as everyone present smiled and laughed when the groom pulled his radiant bride, Midwife Skylar Benton, into his arms for a passionate kiss, something totally out of character for the reserved groom, Dr. Jared Warner.

Midwife Lori Mason tried her best to maintain her own smile as she was a part of the bridal party and it was expected out of her. But sitting there looking on as her friends stared into each other's eyes with an emotion she feared she would never get to feel was becoming harder and harder to do as the night went on. Maybe she would never find that? Maybe she didn't have whatever it was that other people had that could form a bond with someone? At what point did she give up on finding that elusive love and move on with her life, accepting that she was meant to be single? And then what? She'd wanted to be a mother as long as she could remember. If her biological clock was ticking any louder it would drown out the Miranda Lambert song the DJ was playing. Did she just give up on her dream of a family simply because she couldn't find a man who loved her? A man she could trust to always be there for her and their family?

Her old childhood memories of asking her mother why her father didn't love her resurfaced, but she pushed them away. She wasn't looking for a father figure. The time for that had long passed. She wanted someone to share a family with. She wanted children. A family of her own. Was that too much to ask for?

She looked over to where her friend Bree was curled up next to her fiancé with Knox's arms holding her close. They were probably discussing their own wedding just a few months away. It seemed that all her friends were moving forward while she was stuck in the same place she'd been since she had graduated with her midwifery degree. She was even still living in her childhood home, though her mother now spent most of her time where she worked at the Legacy House for pregnant women.

"What's wrong with me?" she asked, only realizing she'd spoken out loud when the man next to her turned toward her. Dr. Zachary Morales, the man who'd agreed to her last-minute invitation to the wedding when Donald, her "plus one," whom she'd been dating for over three months, had suddenly decided that attending a wedding with Lori was "moving things too fast" had been a surprise. After introducing him to her friends before the wedding, he'd quickly fit right in with the group, something her now ex-boyfriend, Donald, had never done. Whether that was because a lot of them shared a medical background she didn't know. What she did know was that when she'd seen Zach dressed in his tailored black tux sitting across the room as she'd walked in with the wedding procession, she had quickly forgotten about her no-show ex.

And what did that say about her? That she'd date a man for months when deep inside she'd always known he wasn't the man for her? And why had she done that? She knew the reason, though she wouldn't admit it to anyone else.

SINGLE DAD'S FAKE FIANCÉE

She'd dated him because she felt safe with him, safe from giving even a small part of her heart to him. She told herself that if he'd been the right one, she would have taken that risk. But would she? How could she know that when she did meet the right man, she'd be brave enough to take that risk?

"I'm not sure what you mean," he said. "Are you not feeling well?"

"There's nothing wrong with you," Bree said from beside her, her friend instinctively knowing what Lori was asking. "Sky said she told you to get rid of Donald the first time she met him."

"She said he didn't look at me the right way. What does that even mean?" Lori asked. Sky always seemed to have a sixth sense about the men that Lori dated. Unfortunately, it was always the opposite of hers.

"Can you please explain what Sky meant?" Bree asked, turning toward her fiancé.

"I'm not an expert, but from what I have seen, when a man is interested in a woman, there can be a million people in a room, but his attention is primarily on that woman. Like the way Jack is looking at Lori's mother right now." Knox nodded his head to a table half-way across the room.

DEANNE ANDERS

Lori glanced over to where her boss and her mother sat, laughing and smiling at each other. When the senior Dr. Warner raised Lori's mom's hand to his lips, Lori looked away quickly. It seemed that everyone in her world was pairing off. That was, everyone except her.

"Let's dance," Bree said, taking Knox's hand and leading him out to the dance floor. Lori watched the couple and smiled. If those two could find each other, surely she could find the right man for her.

"I feel like I'm missing something," Zach said, reminding Lori that she wasn't alone, even though at that moment she felt more alone than she had in her whole life. "Why do you think there's something wrong with you?"

A sudden thought crossed her mind. The only thing she had really known about the new doctor was that he had recently moved to Nashville in the hopes of making a new start in his life after losing his wife the year before. From everything she had heard, Zach had been very devoted to his wife and had taken a long sabbatical before deciding to move his practice from Memphis to Nashville. Lori's invitation to the doctor had been more of a coincidence as he'd just walked up on the OB-GYN floor after

12 SINGLE DAD'S FAKE FIANCÉE

she'd hung up after Donald's phone call leaving her once again to be the third wheel with her friends. She'd explained to Zach that her boyfriend, make that ex-boyfriend, had canceled on her at the last minute. While making sure to keep the disappointment from her voice, she'd asked Zach if he'd like to come with her as a way to make some new connections with the staff. Lori had made it clear that it would in no way be considered as anything other than a chance for her to introduce him to more of his coworkers, and she'd been pleasantly surprised when he'd agreed.

Now, looking at him, pretty much a stranger to her and her friends, she realized she had the one person who might give her an honest opinion on what she was doing wrong.

"Well, let's see. Where should I start?" Lori looked around the room, then nodded, motioning to the head table. "So, the bride and groom over there, Jared and my best friend, Sky, they danced around each other a few months, then bam, head over heels in love. Then there's Bree and Knox. They met at our office while Knox was filling in for another one of our doctors that was on leave. They barely knew each other three months ago, now they're planning their own wedding. And then there's my mother."

"Your mother?" Zach asked as he scanned the room, as if looking for someone he would recognize as Lori's mother.

Lori pointed to where her mother and the senior Dr. Warner had taken to the dance floor.

"Isn't that Dr. Warner, the founder of the Legacy Women's Clinic?" he asked.

"Yes, that's my boss. Well, kind of. Jared is kind of my boss too now. And that's my mother dancing with him. My mom has worked for Legacy House for years, the home Dr. Warner founded to help pregnant women needing a place to stay. The two of them have a professional relationship. My mom was Dr. Warner's wife's best friend before she passed. Then two weeks ago I walk into Legacy House to find the two of them kissing like a couple of teenagers hiding under the football bleachers."

"You don't approve of your mother's relationship with your boss?" The look in Zach's eyes was one of curiosity. Good. If he was able to follow everything up till now, maybe he would be able to help her.

"It's not that I don't approve. My dad took off years ago. He was a long-haul truck driver

14 SINGLE DAD'S FAKE FIANCÉE

who preferred the open road to being tied down with a family. I think I was five the last time he stopped by the house on his way through town. But after the way my father treated her, Mom has never dated. She was definitely not looking for a man in her life. Neither was Sky, at least not a steady one. And Bree? That story is too long to go into, but the last man she would have fallen for would have been Knox. Still, there they all are," Lori said, spreading out both her hands toward the dance floor that was becoming crowded. "And here I sit, the only one of them that has been actively looking for 'Mr. Right' so that I can start a family and I'm the one that will go home alone tonight."

She took a sip of champagne from her glass, needing the courage to ask her next question. Still staring into her glass, she said, "So, I ask again, what is wrong with me?"

She waited a few minutes, hoping he wouldn't give her the same nonsensical answers her friends always gave her. *"It's not you, it's them." "You deserve better than those losers."* And her all-time favorite: *"Your time will come. Just be patient."* But when Zach didn't say anything, she glanced up to find him staring at her with a curiosity that she wasn't prepared for, his brown eyes studying her so hard that she couldn't help but look away. He was probably thinking she was ridiculous and had just answered her own question by asking him, a stranger, such a ridiculous and personal question.

"Never mind, it's a silly question," she said, reaching for the bottle of champagne on the table and topping off her glass.

"No. It's not a silly question. I don't think you're asking the right question though." He held his own glass up for her to fill. "You say you are looking for Mr. Right, but then you say you want to start a family. So which is it? Do you just want a family? Or are you looking for the love of your life? That one and only true love?"

Now it was Lori's turn to stare at Zach like he was being ridiculous. And then she stopped and actually considered what he was asking. The love of her life? Her one and only true love? Did she even believe that type of love existed? It seemed a long time since she'd considered a man for anything besides his husband and father qualifications. Had she given up on finding that one true love he was talking about? If it wasn't for her friends' relationships, would she even believe in it? Had all her failed relationships caused her to focus only on her goal of having a family?

"I don't know," she said honestly.

"Well, maybe that's the problem. I'm not sure I can give you a lot of advice on finding a man to fall in love with. Things between me and my late wife happened when neither of us were looking to fall in love too. But I can tell you that once you find that once in a lifetime type of love, you'll know it. I can also tell you that finding that great love doesn't guarantee that all your dreams will come true. It has a cost. You have to decide if you are willing to pay that price. I know it's not a cost that I want to ever have to pay again."

His wife. He was talking about the price of losing his wife.

"I'm so sorry, I know you must miss your wife terribly," Lori said, then wanted to bite her tongue off. Of course he missed his late wife. And this was a wedding, a happy occasion. She had no business bringing up what she could tell were painful memories to this man, especially here where he had seemed to be enjoying himself earlier. But then all she'd been was a downer all night.

"Would you like to dance?" Lori said, standing suddenly. Zach had been nice enough to agree to accompany her to the wedding of a couple he didn't even know, and so far all she'd done was whine about her own life. And then she had brought up the painful subject of his losing his wife. She had to do better than this. He deserved better than this. They both deserved better than this tonight. Sky and Jared's wedding was supposed to be a happy occasion about them, not about her.

She held her hand out to him.

He hesitated a moment, then stood and took it, giving her a reassuring smile. "I'd love to."

They joined the other couples and for the next hour they danced to everything from classic country to the current hits. They were both breathless by the time they made their way back to their table after line dancing to a popular bar song.

"I can't believe I used to be able to do that for hours," Lori said, reaching for her glass.

"I can't believe we were line dancing next to Mindy and Trey Carter," Zach said, his smile broad, his eyes wide. Something about that smile and his big brown eyes had Lori taking another large gulp of her drink.

"Sky and Jared delivered their son a few months ago and they've been good friends ever since," Lori said, looking at him from the corner of her eyes.

How had she not noticed just how good-looking the new pediatrician was until tonight? They'd worked together several times since he'd come to Nashville as one of the neonatal hospitalists, though tonight was the first time they hadn't been surrounded by crying babies and worried mothers. Still, somehow, she'd never taken a real good look at the man. Maybe because she'd known he was a grieving husband which meant he was off her radar? But that still didn't mean she couldn't appreciate all his tall, dark and deliciousness. She also couldn't deny that the dancing hadn't been all that sent her heart racing.

"Well, it was a lot of fun. I have to thank you for inviting me tonight. I haven't enjoyed myself this much in..." Zach's smile dimmed and Lori knew he was thinking about his wife. "Anyway, thank you for inviting me."

"Thank you for agreeing to come with me— you saved the night for me. I don't think I could have stood to spend another night feeling like the awkward third party."

"I understand. I've had some experience with that myself since I lost Katherine. My friends, they all meant well, but most of our friends are married. It seemed to make things even more painful to be out with them," Zach said, staring down into his half-empty glass.

"And then there is the awkwardness that everyone feels when you talk to someone who has lost someone. I understood why they felt that way—I've been in the same position. You don't know what to say. You don't know if they want to talk about the person they lost or not. So, you pretend that nothing has changed even though you both know it isn't true."

Lori remembered the feeling she'd had when she'd brought up his wife. He'd been so good at listening to her problems, problems that were so miniscule when compared to losing his wife. "I didn't know your wife, but if you ever want to talk about her, I'll be happy to listen."

Zach's smile, though not as bright as before, returned. "I'd like that. Moving to Nashville has been a blessing in some ways, but I'd lived in Memphis my whole life and I do miss my friends."

Lori lifted the champagne bottle and found it empty just as a waiter strolled by offering them a new bottle. Bree and Knox had waved bye to them as they'd left the wedding reception, and it seemed a waste to open a new bottle just for the two of them, but she took it anyway.

She filled her glass and then Zach's. "A toast to new beginnings and new friends."

"To new beginnings, and new friends."

Zach's glass touched hers and they both took a drink.

"I hope you know I mean that," Lori said. "If you want or need to talk about anything, just call me. Or if you need something, let me know."

"You really mean that, don't you?"

"Of course. Besides, after talking to you about my problems with men, you've given me a lot to think about. I'm not sure what I'm going to do, but I know I need to make a change. I've spent the last three years looking for a man that might not exist and it's gotten me nowhere."

Zach took another drink, then set his glass down and pulled out his phone from his suit's inside pocket. "I want to tell you something and I know it's going to sound a bit unconventional, but I think you'll understand when you see this."

Lori watched him as she opened his phone, trying to prepare herself for whatever he could be about to show her. When he finished scrolling on his phone and pushed it over in front of her, she expected to see a picture of the beautiful woman that he was still mourning over. Instead, the face of a darling little boy, around a year old with curly dark hair and big brown eyes stared back at her with a wide smile. She knew that smile. She'd seen it earlier tonight on Zach's face while they were on the dance floor.

"My son, Andres," Zach said as he took his phone back, staring down at the picture of the little boy, his smile proud though it didn't reach his eyes.

"I didn't know you had a son," Lori said. "He's beautiful."

"He's the reason I moved to Nashville—to make a new life for the two of us."

"Nashville is a great place to raise a family. We have a great children's museum and then there is the zoo." Lori had always dreamed of family outings to places like the zoo and the museum with a family of her own.

"He loves the Memphis Zoo. I'll have to take him to the zoo as soon as I can get him here with me," he said.

"What do you mean? Where is he?"

"It's a long story. Right now he's in Memphis with my in-laws, but I'm hoping to get everything set up so that he can be here with me soon. I'm settling into our new home right now and getting his room set up. There's only one thing I need now, and this is where you're going to think my idea is strange." Zach

22   SINGLE DAD'S FAKE FIANCÉE

paused, looking down at the picture a moment longer before putting his phone back in his pocket. "I need a wife. Any chance you're interested?"

CHAPTER TWO

WHEN LORI BURST out in laughter, Zach knew she hadn't taken him seriously. But who could blame her? She had no idea how desperate he was, how much he needed someone's help to fix a situation that he'd created himself.

After his wife's death his brother had warned him against letting his wife's parents take Andres home from the hospital, but at the time it took all he had to just get through the day. The shock of his healthy wife suddenly going into cardiac arrest, only two days after the birth of their son, had crushed him. Even now, almost a year after he'd received the results of her autopsy, he found it hard to believe that a simple, tiny blood clot could destroy all the dreams they'd made for their family. He'd been inconsolable for the first week as he'd navigated through the funeral arrangements. And after the funeral, when he should have taken his son home, it had seemed too cruel to pry the infant from his grieving mother-in-law's arms.

"I have to say, that was definitely not how I saw my first proposal taking place. I'm afraid I envisioned flowers, a bended knee and maybe a ring," Lori said, as she held out her bare ring finger for him to see. It was when she let out a very unladylike giggle, that Zach realized that her champagne glass was empty.

"I'm sorry," she said, her hand coming up to cover her mouth, before she let out another laugh.

Her humor was catching, and he held up a large golden napkin ring to her. "Will this do?"

"It might be a little big, but I think it will work," she said, reaching for it. Taking it in her hand, she placed it on her ring finger, though at least two fingers could have fit inside it, and held it up toward the twinkling lights inside the reception tent.

"It's perfect," she said, continuing to admire the napkin ring on her finger.

Zach noticed the crowd was beginning to thin out. Because Lori had been part of the wedding party, she'd already been there when he'd arrived and he wasn't sure what arrangements she might have made to get home. One thing he was sure of, neither of them would be driving home.

"It looks like the party is ending," he said. "Did you drive here?"

"What? Oh, no. I rode with Bree and Knox. I can call a service to pick me up," Lori said, looking away from the cheap napkin ring she still wore around her finger to where a crowd was gathering. "Oh, we have to go send Sky and Jared off."

Before he could stop her, she sprang out of the chair, almost falling face-first.

"Hold on," he said, taking her arm to steady her as they hurried to follow the bride and groom who were heading down the drive to where a limo waited for them as all their well-wishers waved colorful lights and yelled their congratulations.

Pulling out his phone, he pulled up the app he'd used earlier that evening and requested a ride. "I've ordered us a car."

"Thank you," Lori said, as she wiped at her eyes. "Why do people cry at weddings?"

Taking her arm, he followed the other guests to the center of the curved driveway where several cars were already waiting for the partying guests. He thought about an answer he heard on a sitcom once, but didn't think she'd appreciate it. "Sometimes happiness moves people to tears. There are a lot of emotions that go into a new marriage. First you know they're leaving their old life behind, and sometimes that means friends and family changes too. But at the same time, it's a new beginning for both the bride and the groom. New beginnings can be both scary and exciting too and everyone responds differently to both."

"Are you excited about coming to Nashville for a new beginning?" Lori asked, her head coming to rest on his shoulder, something that would have made him uncomfortable a few hours ago, but which felt perfectly normal after spending the last few hours with her.

"I'm excited about the possibilities, of course, but mostly I just want to have my son with me." His phone dinged letting him know their driver was only a couple minutes away.

"I still don't understand. Why didn't he move with you? I know that being a single dad in a new city has to be stressful. If you need the recommendation of a good nanny or daycare, I'm sure someone at our office could help you out. With all the mothers that go in and out of our office, I'm sure we could find someone you could trust."

He loved that she included herself in helping

DEANNE ANDERS

him. If only things were that simple. "Things are complicated. My in-laws back in Memphis have been caring for Andres since he was born and they are—" how did he say this without sounding like a bitter son-in-law "—possessive. But we're going to work it out."

Oh, yes, they were certainly working it out. At this rate he'd be lucky if he had his son in Nashville by the time Andres started kindergarten. Or even later.

But it's your fault, he reminded himself. He'd let things get out of hand immediately after his wife's funeral. Instead of standing up and taking control as he should have, he'd all but handed over his infant son to them, something that he was too ashamed to admit to Lori. He'd been a poor example of a father, but that was going to change. Once he had settled Andres home with him, he'd never let his son down again.

A small blue sedan pulled up and Zach led Lori to the car, settling her into the back seat before joining her. The driver repeated Zach's address and started down the driveway.

"Are you okay if we make another stop on the way?" Zach asked the driver.

"Sure, I can add it into the app," the driver said. "Where to?"

28   SINGLE DAD'S FAKE FIANCÉE

"Lori?" Zach asked, easing her back from his shoulder. With her eyes closed and mouth half open, a cute snore sounded in his ear. "Lori, wake up. I need your address."

Another snore escaped her mouth, before she turned toward him and burrowed into his suit jacket. Not sure what to do, he shook her once, but only got a wince and a mumble from her. There was nothing else for him to do. It looked like Lori wouldn't be going home alone after all.

Lori rubbed her face against her pillow. There was something jabbing her in the hip, but she just didn't have the energy to move away from it. Maybe it was time for her to get a new mattress. One of those that cushioned you instead of poked you until you had no choice but to change positions. Rolling over, she felt something cold and metal come to rest against her leg. Reaching down, she pulled out the object, ready to throw it off the bed. Only when the cold metal touched her fingers did she realize what it was. It was the ring. The metal napkin ring Zach had "proposed" with. She slowly opened one eye. Nope, this wasn't her bed.

So where was she? And what had she done?

Afraid of what she might find, she looked to

her left side, but there was no one there. She was alone and from what she could tell by the smooth sheets and undented pillow next to her, she'd been alone all night. Pulling back the sheets, she was relieved to see that she still wore the tea-length bridesmaid dress from the night before. Only her shoes were missing.

The door to the attached bathroom opened, and Zach stepped out. Only this wasn't the white lab-coated Dr. Morales she was used to, or the black-tie–dressed Zach she'd danced with the night before. No, this was a hot, steamy, version of Zachary Morales that made her breath catch.

His dark hair was brushed back, still damp enough that a drop of water rolled down the side of his face. She bit down on her bottom lip before her tongue could sweep out as she felt an uncontrollable need to lick that singular drop. Instead, her eyes followed the drop as it ran down his neck before disappearing into a bare chest that had her biting down even harder. With only a pair of sweatpants hung low on his hips, the man was every woman's dirty dream come true.

But this wasn't a dream. This was real. And somehow, though the headache that had begun to throb behind her temples made it hard to think, she had to figure out how she'd come to spend the night in Zach's bed. Was this even his bed? His house? Her head throbbed again and she remembered all that wonderful champagne she'd drunk the night before and wondered exactly what trouble it had gotten her into.

She looked over to the other side of the bed again. Was it possible that Zach had made his side of the bed after he'd gotten up? And the ring, that stupid napkin ring? Why was it here? He hadn't really been serious about his proposal. Had he?

"Good morning," Zach said as he began to dry his hair with a towel she hadn't noticed. "How are you feeling?"

"Maybe a little like Alice in Wonderland, who shouldn't have drunk that potion?" she said.

"I'm sorry. I didn't realize you'd…enjoyed… so much of the champagne till we were headed home. I couldn't get you to wake up to get your address so I brought you here with me. I hope you're okay with that."

"Of course. I'm sorry I put you in that position. I guess I shouldn't have been complaining about being the only one of my friends going home alone." She thought about what she said. "Not that I did this on purpose."

Dropping the towel on his dresser, he opened a drawer and pulled out a dark blue T-shirt. He pulled it over his head, giving her a view of taut muscles that had her stretching her neck to get a closer view.

"I didn't think you did," he said, turning back toward her. "It's fine. I have four bedrooms, but this is the only one with a bed so far, so I took the couch."

He walked into the closet and came out carrying a white pullover. "I was about to start breakfast."

Lori pushed the sheets off and climbed out of bed, then began to look for her shoes, locating one beside the bed. "I've been enough trouble. I'll call for a ride."

"You weren't any trouble at all. Let me show you my appreciation for inviting me last night with some eggs and bacon. It will help you feel better too," he said as he headed out the door. "The kitchen is downstairs on the left."

Waiting till he'd left, she got down on her knees and located her other shoe. Slipping both of them on, she looked from the bedroom door to the bathroom. Scooping her purse up from where she'd seen it lying on the dresser, she

32 SINGLE DAD'S FAKE FIANCÉE

rushed into the bathroom to freshen up. She just hoped that a cold splash of water would be enough to cool down all her overstimulated hormones that Zach Morales had just awakened.

The smell of bacon was working its way upstairs by the time she came out of the bathroom. Not being much of a drinker normally, she wasn't sure how her stomach would handle eating, but right then her stomach growled at the delicious smell, so eggs and bacon it would be.

"Have a seat," Zachary said when she entered the modern kitchen set up with a long island facing windows that showed a large fenced back yard with a small playhouse and a swing set. She suspected that it hurt Zach every time he looked out that window and thought of his son not being there.

"How do you like your eggs?" Zach asked. "I can do scrambled and scrambled."

"I guess I'll go with the scrambled. How about I make some toast?"

"Perfect," he said, pointing toward the pantry.

They worked in silence, neither feeling the need to talk. Then they sat side by side and there was no awkwardness there either, though Lori did find her eyes straying to him whenever he wasn't looking. Still, even with this new awareness that she felt around him, there was a comfortable feeling between them that Lori knew was rare. As rare as the friendships she had with Sky and Bree.

"Tell me about your son," she asked, wanting to know more about the cute toddler with the eyes and smile that matched his father's.

"He's a happy child, for that I'm thankful," he said.

"You were afraid he wouldn't be? Because of the loss of his mother?" she asked before standing to bring the coffeepot closer. "And what's this thing with your in-laws? Explain it all to me again."

She was afraid she'd crossed the line when she poured coffee into his cup and noticed the white-knuckled hold he had on it. Whatever it was, why ever he felt he needed to have a wife to bring his son to Nashville to live with him, she wanted to know. And if there was anything she could do to help him within her power, with the exception of marrying him, she'd do it.

His hand moved away from his cup, and he put his fork down before turning toward her. Any of the comfort she'd felt between them was gone. He had withdrawn from her, as if explaining about his son would change things between them. But why?

"When Katherine died, I was a mess. By the time I started getting myself together, my son had been with my in-laws for a couple months." He looked down at his half-eaten plate of food. "Andres was so little and I felt so alone and unable to cope without his mother. So, I took the easy way out. I let him stay with his grandparents, thinking that it was what was best for him to have us all around him."

He looked up to her, his eyes searching hers. For what? Did he really think she was going to judge him for his actions? Why? Because she'd told him how her own father had left her? He had to know that this wasn't the same. He'd just been through the trauma of losing his wife. How could she judge him? How could anyone? He was grieving. And the truth was, at that time it might have been better for his son to stay with his grandparents. Who was she or anyone else to judge that? Who else could know what he was able to handle at that time, but Zach?

"You needed time to grieve. I understand that. And it's understandable that you needed some time to come to terms with being a single dad. A new baby is a lot for anyone, especially someone who has just lost their wife."

"But I'm a pediatrician. I should have been able to handle it."

"No. You were a man who had just lost his partner. You were a new father that felt overwhelmed." She held her hand up when he would have interrupted her. "You were in shock. It's understandable and I'm sure it's not the first time that grandparents have stepped in and helped this way. I've had patients, couples, that go stay with their family members the first few weeks, just so they have that extra support."

"Besides, all of that is in the past," she went on before he could try to interrupt her again. It was plain to see that he was suffering a terrible case of guilt. It would take time for him to get over it. The only thing that would help was for him to put things right with his son now. Which meant he had to move forward. "Now, tell me the reason, the real reason, your son is not here with you now."

He looked at her, stunned. Was he so used to the people in his life judging him for what he'd done? "You don't understand. I did this. I wasn't the father I should have been."

"From what I can see, you did exactly what a

36 SINGLE DAD'S FAKE FIANCÉE

caring father would have done. You knew you couldn't take care of your son, so you put him with people you trusted. You were doing the best you could. You're human. Give yourself a break. What matters now is getting your son back with you, right?"

He stared at her, his brown eyes studying her as if he wasn't sure he could believe her words. "You understand."

"Yes, I do," Lori said. "Now, tell me what we need to do to get your son here with you, where he belongs."

They cleared the table as they talked, him explaining his relationship with his in-laws, which seemed to have been good until he'd told them that he was moving to Nashville to make a new life for him and his son. As could be expected from doting grandparents, the thought of not seeing their grandson daily had not gone over well.

"Did you consider just taking Andres to live with you instead of moving out of town?"

"Oh, I tried to do that just weeks after he was born, but there was always a reason that my mother-in-law didn't feel that it would work. First it was that my hours were too irregular— a baby needed consistency. My answer to that was to get a live-in nanny. Her answer to that was why do that, when I could just move in with them."

"Oh, no. Tell me you didn't do that." She handed him a plate to load into the dishwasher, then took a kitchen rag and began wiping down the stove.

"Of course I did. But even though I was still in the same house with my son, I was made to feel like a visitor. Like someone they were allowing to spend time with his own son. That's when I talked to my brother and decided to relocate my practice to Nashville."

It must have been really bad for him to go to the extreme of relocating his practice, which was not only a lot of work, but expensive too. He had to have felt that it was his only choice.

"I still don't understand why you don't just go to their house and take your son. You're his father."

Zach placed the last of the dishes in the dishwasher and turned it on before answering her. "My wife was an only child. They doted on her and she loved them very much. I know that I wasn't the only one that suffered a loss when she died. Over the years that Katherine and I dated, then married, I came to love them too. I lost my parents when I was nine. My older brother and I went to live with my cousins, but

38 SINGLE DAD'S FAKE FIANCÉE

it wasn't the same. Katherine's parents came to be like a new set of parents to me. We were as close as families could be until now."

So not only had he lost his wife, now he feared he was going to lose the love of his in-laws, people who he'd thought loved him like a son. The longer his story went on, the sadder it was becoming.

"And you're right. When I let them take Andres home from the hospital, I had no doubt he was in good hands. But now, they aren't the same. It's like instead of accepting that they lost their daughter, they have used Andres to fill that hole in their hearts. Anytime I've mentioned taking Andres, made plans to move out on my own with him, they've countered with reasons why that wouldn't work out. Katherine's death changed them, especially her mother. This last time, when I explained that I was moving to Nashville, they threatened to take me to court. To say that I had abandoned my son. They're threatening to file for custody."

It was easy to see the hurt in his eyes. "If I have to go to court, I will. But I would rather find another way. Some way to counteract all their reasons for why a single dad with a demanding job can't give their grandson as good of a life as they can."

"So, you weren't joking about needing a wife?" The whole idea that he would just marry some stranger still sounded absurd to her. Of course, if you considered that she'd realized just the night before that she'd spent the last three years looking for a baby's daddy more than for a man that would love her, maybe she shouldn't be so judgmental.

"I know they're going to try to show that as a single dad with a demanding job, Andres is better off with them. They can probably use the fact that I left him with them after Katherine passed as evidence that I, myself, didn't even think I could take care of him."

She could see why he'd think that having a wife, someone to share in taking care of his son might help, but there were a lot of single moms doing fine raising their children. That reasoning wouldn't get them far. And it would be hard to argue that Zach wasn't moving forward, hadn't dealt with his grief and wasn't ready to be a fulltime parent to his son, if he was to marry. But Lori thought that what Zach needed more than anything was to have someone on his side. To show his in-laws that he had someone in his corner that was ready to go head-to-head with them and that would be there for Andres too. And Zach needed to know that he wasn't alone. Lori could tell with just the little amount of time that she'd spent with him that, though he did have a brother and cousins, Zach had been bearing this burden alone for a long time.

"You said you have a brother? He lives here?" she asked. Having family support nearby would be a plus too.

"He's lives in Hendersonville, so about thirty minutes away. He and his wife have three kids, the youngest is just a month older than Andres."

"Well, that's good. I'm sure Andres's grandparents want him to grow up around family." Lori washed out the dishrag and spread it out to dry. "And even if they don't, I'm sure a judge would take your having family support into consideration too."

"I'm hoping it doesn't go that far. I know we are at odds now about what is best for my son, but there was a time when I thought of them as family too." He turned to her, his eyes sober. "I don't want to hurt my wife's parents. She loved them and I know she'd never want me to hurt them this way. I have to find a way to make everything right between us, but still have my son here with me where he belongs. Does that make sense?"

It made perfect sense, and just showed what type of man he truly was. He was the kind of man she had been looking for, one that would make a great father.

Only he wasn't looking for a wife to love, he was looking for a wife to take care of his son. It would be a ready-made family, something that might have been tempting to her if she hadn't seen that sad look in his eyes every time he talked about his wife. It was one thing to give up on finding her Mr. Right. It was a whole other thing to live in the shadow of a woman who was no longer here in this world. No, that was not something that any woman should ever have to do.

And though she didn't agree with what his in-laws were doing, she had never met them. They might normally be perfectly nice people. Life had changed for all of them the moment Zach's wife, their only daughter, had died, and that had apparently changed the dynamics of their relationship too. But maybe there was still hope for them, if not for their sake, for the sake of the little boy who they all loved.

They'd busied themselves as they'd talked and the kitchen now was spotless. It was time

42 SINGLE DAD'S FAKE FIANCÉE

for Lori to go, but her mind kept going over and over Zach's problem. Problem solving had always been something she enjoyed. It was one of the things that had drawn her into going to nursing school.

"So, what if instead of going to the extreme of marrying someone, which I think would be a terrible idea, you make your in-laws think you're getting married." She sat down on one of the bar stools. Her headache had retreated to the back of her neck now and though the food had helped her stomach settle, she was still feeling some of the effects of her over-partying.

"What do you mean?" he said, leaning against the island that separated them. "Make up a story about some woman I'm engaged to? And when they want to meet her? They'd be even more determined to keep Andres if they believed I would try to fool them."

"I'm not saying make up someone. Haven't you ever read a romance novel?"

One dark eyebrow went up at her question. Why wasn't she surprised?

"Okay, here's a quick tutorial. First, romance books are a great genre, and every man should at least read one before they count them out. Second, a lot—I'd say the majority—of romance books have tropes, certain themes or plots that readers love. One of the most popular ones, and one of my favorites, is the fake fiancée trope."

Zach leaned in closer. "You read those books?"

"I love those books. And I think they could hold the answer to your problem."

He took a seat across from her and waited.

"Okay, so how these books work is, someone, say a billionaire or a—" she pointed to him "—single dad, needs a wife. Sometimes it's because of family issues, such as nagging parents who refuse to quit matchmaking. Sometimes it's a business arrangement. Sometimes it's just to save someone from being humiliated, like when someone's ex is getting married and they've been invited to the wedding."

"I'd say they're all silly ideas, except I can feel where they are coming from. So, what exactly do they do to make people believe them? It isn't like you can suddenly show up with a fiancée and no one is going to be suspicious."

Lori looked at him before making a dramatic eye roll. "Your plan was to show up with a *wife* that no one had ever heard of. You didn't think that might look a little suspicious?"

Zach's lips parted in a smile. "I admit, it

wasn't something I had thought out. It's just that we were talking about you needing a husband and a family and it just seemed like me having a wife would help out with my in-laws concerns about me being a single dad. But you're right. This sounds like a much better idea."

"Of course it does," she said, smiling back at him smugly.

"But those books you're talking about, with this fake fiancée trope. They're romances, so that means they always end with a happy ending, right? Boy gets the girl, that kind of thing?"

"Well, yes. But in this case, instead of a romantic happy ending, you'll have a happy ending with your son." Lori felt a little tinge of uneasiness. She knew exactly how those stories ended. The single dad not only ended up with the son, but also with the girl. Only from the way Zach had looked every time he talked about his late wife, the last thing he would want was to end up with the girl. He'd made it plain that he thought the cost of love was too high the night of Sky's wedding.

"So, you'll do it?" he asked, his smile so confident that she almost agreed.

"Why me?" She knew she should be shocked

by his request, but it had been her idea and she had to admit she had been considering it the whole time she'd been explaining it to him. Her life was at a standstill and it didn't look like he had anyone else that could do that for him. Maybe just pretending to be engaged would help her discover what it was she was going to do with her life. She'd always thought that she would have that happily-ever-after that she read about. But right now she wasn't sure that would ever be in her future. At least it wasn't unless she made some changes and found some way to trust her heart, something that she had never been able to do.

And then there were those big brown eyes. Not only the ones that stared at her so hopefully right then, but the ones of the little boy in the picture Zach had showed her. In her heart she knew those two belonged together. And unlike her father, Zach was trying to do the right thing for his son.

But playing as Zach's fiancée? She was still recovering from her reaction to him this morning in the bedroom. Playing his fiancée, spending the amount of time with him that would entail, could be dangerous, at least for her.

"Who better? You seem to be an expert on this faking thing," Zach said.

"I'm certainly not an expert at faking it. It's not like it's something I've ever done." But hadn't she done just that through relationship after relationship? Pretending that she wanted to love and be loved, while the whole time a part of her was self-consciously waiting for the person she was involved with to leave her? She could even see now that she'd been the one to end relationships because of her fear that if she got too close to someone she was afraid they were going to leave her. Hadn't Skye accused her of running away from people when they got too close?

"But you know how to, you've read about it. You'd make a perfect fiancée," Zach said, so confident that she was beginning to believe him.

"I'm perfect because I'm the only woman you know in Nashville." She understood she was too close to agreeing with him. She needed to stop and think this out.

"You're perfect because you're the only one I trust," Zach said.

Somehow she realized, deep inside herself, that he meant those words. They barely knew each other, yet he trusted her. It sounded unbelievable after the short period of time they'd known each other, but she felt the same way.

Too bad she trusted the one man that wasn't available. Or maybe that was why she felt safe trusting him.

That realization had her standing and walking over to the counter where she'd laid her purse. She needed to leave before she agreed. She needed to think things over and make sure that she was up to this. The last thing she wanted to do was to fail to help Zach get his son back. Or even worse, make things even more difficult for him. "I need to think about it. See if I can make it work."

"But you are going to think about it?" His eyes lit up with hope, making it even harder for her to walk away without giving him an answer.

Oh, she was definitely thinking about it, thinking how she could help him convince his in-laws that his son belonged with his father and his wife-to-be. If only it was that simple.

Because there was one thing she hadn't told Zach about those romance books that she had read, the hero and heroine always got their happily-ever-after. But with a man who was still grieving the loss of his wife, the only happily-ever-after she could hope for in this case was for the hero to get his son back.

CHAPTER THREE

ZACH WATCHED AS Lori walked up the sidewalk to her house. He wasn't sure what to think of the midwife. He didn't think he'd ever met anyone quite like her before. She had so much energy and she was so spontaneous, something she would have to be to consider his proposal of faking an engagement with him.

A fake engagement. What had he been thinking? He didn't even know if it would help him with his situation with his in-laws, but then it couldn't hurt. And he wasn't sure why, but for some reason, he felt that having Lori by his side was just what he needed. It just seemed right.

A pang of guilt rushed over him. It was supposed to be Katherine by his side, not a woman that he barely knew. The fact that he was even considering letting someone get close to him like this made him uncomfortable. He had no right to be forming a relationship, even a platonic one with Lori.

But how was he supposed to make this all work? How was he supposed to pretend to be in a relationship with Lori? A part of him had been frozen since the moment he lost his wife. He had no idea how to even act intimate with another woman now, though he had to say, he and Lori did have a surprising chemistry together. And there was that guilt again. He shouldn't be feeling an type of chemistry for Lori. But there it was. Would it make it easier to pull off this whole pretense?

After leaving the house, Zach headed to the nearest bookstore. Maybe Lori was right. Maybe he did need to read some of those romance books she was talking about.

Zach had just dropped Lori off at her home when her phone rang. It was her mother, not surprising since she'd already noticed her mom's car at the curb.

"Where are you?" her mother asked.

Lori looked down at the bridesmaid dress that she still wore and for a second Lori considered calling Zach and having him come back and get her. She knew her mother was going

50 SINGLE DAD'S FAKE FIANCÉE

to assume that she'd spent the night with the new doctor Lori had invited to the wedding.

This was going to be as awkward as catching her boss and her mother play tonsil hockey on the family couch, a picture that would be burned in her brain for eternity.

Well, it seemed now would be as good a time as any to try out her acting skills. If nothing else, she could at least hint that there was something going on between her and Zach. That wasn't a lie. At least there could be soon if she agreed to help him.

Was she really thinking about doing this with Zach? Fake an engagement with someone she barely knew? What was she thinking?

Well, that was easy. She was thinking about helping a man who'd already lost his wife and was in danger of losing his son. She would hope that someone would have helped her father if he'd wanted to get back into Lori's life, though she'd given up on that dream years ago.

"I'm here," she said as she opened the door to their home. "I thought it was your weekend to stay at Legacy House."

Her mother hung up the phone as Lori walked into the foyer, stopping when she saw Lori as her eyes swept up and down her daughter. "You haven't been home since the wedding?"

"Since you would know that if you had spent the night here, I guess I could ask you the same question." Lori wasn't an amateur when it came to getting out of trouble with her mom. Changing the subject had always worked well for her. Putting her mom on the defense wouldn't hurt either.

"I've been here. Your car was in the garage so I figured you were home," her mother said, ignoring the fact that Lori knew her mother would have checked in on her in her room if she had actually come in during the night.

"Okay. You caught me. I spent the night at Zach's place." Lori realized her mom would read more into that statement than she should, but it was the truth. Her mother probably wouldn't even believe her if she told her there had been nothing but sleeping going on at Zach's.

"Jack introduced me to Dr. Morales before the wedding. He seems like a nice guy, especially compared to Donald."

Had anyone liked her ex? Now that she thought about it, she hadn't given the man one thought once she'd begun talking to Zach the night before.

"He is really a nice guy. I'm glad I invited him." Lori moved past her mother, heading up the stairs to shower and change.

"Just be careful, Lori. Jack said Zach lost his wife just over a year ago. I don't want to see you hurt."

Lori stopped and turned toward her mom. Part of her wanted to tell her all about Zach's issues with his in-laws and his son. But that wasn't her story to tell, even though she'd love her mother's advice.

And if she did decide to play the part of Zach's fiancée, she wouldn't be able to tell anyone, not even her mother. For all practical purposes, she'd be his fiancée. It had to be that way if they wanted to make sure he got his son back. "Don't worry, Mom. Things are good between us. I feel like I've known him all my life, and I think he feels the same way."

And that part wasn't a lie. Hopefully, that would just be one more thing that would help them be successful if she agreed to help him. Lori started up the stairs then stopped.

"Mom, is that why you haven't dated anyone till now? Because you were grieving over Jim leaving?" She'd refused to call her father by anything but his given name since she'd been a teenager and sent him a letter he'd never answered back.

"Grieving? No, I wouldn't say that. I think it was more that I lost the ability to trust someone not to hurt me again."

Lori hadn't been sure how she felt about her mother dating her boss until then. If there was anyone she knew that would never hurt her mother, it would be Dr. Warner. But it had taken her mom twenty years to get to the point that she could trust another man. Lori couldn't help but think of herself twenty years from now, still single, still childless. Still waiting for a man she could trust enough to have the kind of relationship her friends had. "I'm happy for you and Dr. Warner. And I know that you can trust him."

The office was short with both a midwife and a doctor being off and it would stay that way until Sky and Jared were back from their honeymoon. But while everyone had their hands full, there was still talk of the weekend wedding. Lori wasn't surprised when she was stopped by several of the staff with questions about the new guy she'd brought to the wedding. Their office was a close group, but they also had their share of gossips so she'd prepared herself with noncommittal answers concerning her and Zach, while still leaving them with a hint that she was interested in getting to know the new doctor at the hospital better. When she found herself cornered by the office receptionist, the lifeline to the office rumor mill, she more than hinted that she and Zach planned to be seeing more of each other.

"I hear he lost his wife last year," he said. "Don't go and get yourself hurt, girl."

She'd just laughed and brushed off the comment. The people she worked with knew her record of picking the wrong man almost every time. "He's a nice guy and he's new to town. I just want him to feel...welcomed."

She winked at him and walked away. That would surely cause some whispers around the clinic. It might even become more popular than the one concerning her mother and the senior Dr. Warner. Besides, it couldn't hurt to have the staff thinking of the two of them as interested in each other.

Because though she still hadn't given her answer to Zach's request, she knew that she was leaning toward agreeing to play his fake fiancée. Zach needed her help. So did the little boy who had no mother. And it wasn't as if she had anything else going on in her life. She had no love life. And after talking with her mother and looking back over her history with men, she wasn't even sure now that it was something she would ever be ready for. Still, accepting the possibility that she'd never meet her Mr. Right was hard for her. Just as hard as accepting that she might never have the family, the children, that she'd always dreamed of having.

Her workload was heavy that morning, so it was lunchtime before she could round on the patients that had delivered over the weekend and she was nervous about the possibility of running into Zach. He would want an answer soon and she still worried that she wouldn't be able to do what he needed her to do. Just the fact that the clinic's receptionist had considered that Zach would be interested in her surprised her.

Because, while Zach with his dark and mysterious vibes would draw women to him by groves, she was just a plain Jane, nothing special at all. With her pale skin and light brown hair, she definitely wasn't the type of woman that a man would suddenly declare his undying love for or his plans to marry her. How were they supposed to make anyone, especially his in-laws, suddenly believe in their love at first sight?

56   SINGLE DAD'S FAKE FIANCÉE

She was so busy thinking about Zach and his in-laws, that she didn't hear the nurse's call for help until the nurse passed Lori with a woman in the wheelchair. The woman's panting and white-knuckled grip on the arms of the wheelchair was proof enough for both of them that this woman was in labor.

"What room?" Lori asked, running in front of Sandy, one of the more experienced nurses on the unit.

"Room eight, it should be set up for an emergency delivery," Sandy said.

Lori ran to the room and opened the door, holding it open for the nurse. It took both of them to help the woman into the bed. And as Sandy began to undress their patient, Lori pulled the emergency call light, then returned to the woman's side.

"My name is Lori. I'm one of the midwives here on the unit. Can you tell me the name of your OB doctor?"

"I haven't seen one," the woman said before her hands grabbed ahold of the bed's side rails and she began to bear down.

"Try not to push," Lori told her, though she knew the woman was too far into the contraction to listen to her.

Another nurse rushed into the room as Lori

grabbed a pair of gloves. It took just a moment for Lori to confirm that not only was the woman in active labor, but she was only minutes from delivering. The good news was that Lori was sure that the baby was coming headfirst, as she could already see a dark cap of hair as it began to crown. "Call and see if there is an OB doc on the floor."

Without any prenatal care, Lori had no idea what complications she could be facing with the delivery or with the baby after delivery. She didn't even know if this baby was term. "And call the nursery, have them send down the NICU team."

"I know this is hard—" heavens, Lori didn't even know this woman's name "—but it's almost over. We're trying to get one of the doctors into the room in case there are complications, so try not to push if you can."

The woman took a breath and began to bear down again and Lori knew there would be no waiting for a doctor. She'd be the one delivering this baby.

"What's your name?" Lori asked the woman when she stopped to take a breath.

"It doesn't matter," the woman said, her eyes avoiding Lori's, causing a chill to run down her back. Something was definitely wrong here.

58   SINGLE DAD'S FAKE FIANCÉE

But as the woman bore down again, Lori had to put everything else aside as she carefully delivered a small dark-haired head, then one shoulder and then the other one. The NICU team arrived just in time as she delivered the rest of the body, then held the tiny newborn only a moment, drying it off, before it let out a weak cry. Quickly clamping and cutting the cord, Lori handed the baby to one of the NICU nurses. By the small size of the baby girl, weighing no more than five pounds if she had to guess, the baby looked to be at least six weeks premature.

The door opened and Zach came into the room. Their eyes only met for a moment before he headed toward the neonatal unit where he took control of the assessment. While Lori finished with the delivery and a small repair, she listened to Zach as he began his assessment.

"One-minute Apgar?" he asked one of the nurses assisting him.

"I gave her a seven, counting off for her tone, reflex and color."

"Her Dubowitz is coming out at around thirty-four weeks. Lori, what was her due date?" he asked.

Lori looked at her patient, but the woman turned her gaze away from her. Whether from

DEANNE ANDERS

guilt about not getting any prenatal care or simply not caring, Lori wasn't sure. Something was definitely wrong with this situation and Lori would be having a conversation with this mother as soon as they had more privacy. "There was no prenatal care, so I'm not sure."

A buzzer went off and one of the NICU nurses silenced it. "Five-minute Apgar score of eight. Still some cyanosis, but she has a heart rate of one hundred and forty, good flexion and respiratory effort with a good cry, though she's breathing a little fast and her tone could be better."

"Breath sounds are good, and I don't hear any murmur. Let's get her to the NICU and get a preterm blood panel," Zach said.

As Lori and Sandy repositioned the patient, who still hadn't disclosed her name, Zach walked over to the bed to join them. "I'm Dr. Morales. I'm the pediatric and neonatal hospitalist here at the hospital. It looks like your little girl came a few weeks early, but she seems to be handling it well. We're going to watch her closely in the NICU for the next few hours. Do you have any questions for me?"

When the woman didn't say anything, he went on, "Lori and the nurses are going to want to get your medical history so that we

60 SINGLE DAD'S FAKE FIANCÉE

can know if there is anything we should be worried about. Some of those questions might be personal, but they're important for us to care for your baby. We're not here to judge you. We just want you and your baby to get the best care possible." Zach nodded to Lori and Sandy before leaving the room. Whether he'd seen the marks on the woman's arms or whether he just had good intuition, Lori knew he suspected the same thing as she did. The most probable reason this woman hadn't gotten prenatal care was because she was using drugs. Which meant the little baby girl that Lori had just delivered was not only a few weeks premature, she would probably also have to go through drug withdrawal.

"Sandy, if you could get...?" Lori said, hoping to force the woman to give them some type of identification.

"You can call me Christy," the woman said before turning away from them. "I don't need anything. I'm just tired and need to sleep."

"How about we let you rest for an hour, and then I'll be back to check on you? We'll get you some food brought up too. Sound like a plan?"

The woman shrugged her shoulders and Lori and Sandy slipped out of the room, closing the door quietly behind them.

"Do you think her name is really Christy?" Sandy asked.

"I don't know," Lori said, "but I hope to find out. She has to realize that we aren't going to send that baby home with her without getting her information."

"From the needle marks on her arms, I don't think that baby will be going home with her at all. I don't know if she noticed that I drew some blood when I started her IV. I'll add a drug toxicology screening to the prenatal panel."

"Let me know when you get the results. I've got three postpartum patients to see on the floor and then I'm going to go by NICU and check on the baby before I head back to the office." While Sandy headed toward the nurse's station, Lori stopped at her first patient's room.

In forty minutes, she had seen all three patients and written discharge orders on two of them. By the time she made it to the NICU department, she had fifteen minutes left. She knew there was nothing she could do for the little girl she'd just delivered, but she felt this overwhelming need to make sure that the baby was doing well. Maybe it was because the baby's mother had shown no interest in her. The thought of a baby all alone in this big new world without her momma's arms to comfort her tore at Lori's heart when her own arms ached to hold a child of her own.

"How's she doing?" she asked Zach as she came up behind him. While there were several babies in warmers and isolettes, she recognized the baby she had just delivered immediately. She had a tiny nasal cannula in her equally tiny nose and another tiny intravenous catheter had been inserted into her arm with a small two-hundred-and-fifty-milligram bag of fluid running into it. While the baby's color had improved, Lori could see that she was still breathing too fast.

"Did the mother tell you when her water broke?" he asked, all his attention on the baby.

"No. She's not cooperating at all. I couldn't even get a last name from her. I do know it had broken before she came into the hospital. We agreed to let her sleep for an hour and then talk. We ordered a toxicology screen with the regular labs and I'm sure it will come back positive, I just don't know with what." Lori leaned over the warmer and placed her finger in the baby's hand. When her little hand grasped her finger, hanging on tightly, Lori's heart broke. This little one would be a fighter whether her mother cared or not. Right then, she decided no matter what, she was going to make sure this child got the love and the care she needed so badly.

Lori carefully removed her finger from the delicate little hand. "I'll let you know what I find out as soon as I finish talking to her."

The door to the NICU unit opened and Sandy rushed in. One look at her strained face and Lori realized something was very wrong.

"She's gone," Sandy said, her face pale and her breathing labored as if she'd run all the way from the patient's room.

It only took a minute for Lori to realize who she was talking about. "Christy? Do you have security looking for her?"

"I can't," Sandy said, holding out a piece of paper to Lori.

Lori recognized the sheet of paper as one of the information letters that the hospital had placed in every patient's room, but when she turned it over, she saw what it was that had upset Sandy.

"'To whom it concerns, I am leaving the hospital and I am leaving my baby under the Tennessee Safe Haven law. Please take care of her. I am doing this of my own free will and according to this law I cannot be prosecuted,'" Lori read, then handed the letter to Zach.

64 SINGLE DAD'S FAKE FIANCÉE

"She can do this?" one of the NICU nurses asked.

"Yes, within two weeks of birth," Zach answered. "The law was put in place to protect the baby and also the privacy of the parents."

"Better that a baby is given up somewhere safe, like a hospital, than just abandoned on the street," Sandy said, though you could tell she was still upset.

"It's okay. It's not your fault. I should have insisted that she talk to me right away instead of waiting," Lori said. "Maybe I could have found out what was going on and found her some help before she did something this desperate."

"It wouldn't have mattered. She never intended to answer your questions when she came into the hospital. This was probably her plan all the time. The good thing is we did get some lab work before she left. And so far, this little one seems to be holding her own. All we can do is take care of her for right now," Zach said.

"I'll call DCS," Sandy said. "They can open a case immediately and hopefully there will be someone special out there who will love that little baby just as if it was their own."

"No, I'll make the call," Lori said, her mind

already spinning with possibilities. Possibilities that had her heart beating fast and her hopes soaring to the sky. Here was a baby that had been abandoned. A baby that needed a mother to love her. Lori knew how it felt to be abandoned. No child ever deserved to feel unwanted. It was as if all the puzzle pieces of her life, the ones she had been struggling with, were suddenly falling into place. She'd thought about adoption before and had been involved with several patients that had chosen adoptive families for their babies. She'd considered that it might be something she wanted to do in the future. But delivering this baby and then just as fast discovering that the tiny girl had been abandoned—it was as if it was meant to be now.

"How about coffee later?" Zach asked as Lori was heading out to make the call. She could tell he wanted to know her answer about helping him.

For just a moment, she studied him. She knew so little about the man, yet it was everything she needed to know.

She'd seen how gentle he could be as he had carefully examined the newborn. She'd seen how patient he was with the mother of the newborn, showing no judgment for the fact that the woman hadn't received the proper maternity care. And she'd seen the way his eyes lit up when he talked about his son.

How could she not help a man like Zach, one that would be there to help her if she ever needed it? "How about we meet as soon as I finish at the office? I think the two of us have a lot to talk about."

CHAPTER FOUR

AFTER RECEIVING A text saying that she was free to meet him, Zach waited in the hospital café for her to join him while he went over the call he'd just received from his mother-in-law inviting him down for the weekend. Inviting him to see his own son? He felt anger boiling up inside him.

He'd been a patient man. Oh, he'd messed up by not taking on the responsibility of his newborn son when his wife had died, though what else was he supposed to do when his grieving mother-in-law kept reminding him over and over that his son needed someone who'd had experience with a newborn? Somehow between his own grief and her assurance that it was the best thing for Andres to go home with her, the fact that he was a pediatrician seemed to be ignored.

But his anger cooled when he remembered his mother-in-law's silence when he had told

68 SINGLE DAD'S FAKE FIANCÉE

her he might be bringing someone with him, someone he wanted her to meet. It took a lot to shut the woman up, but that had done it. She'd had the same reaction when he'd told her he was moving to Nashville and would be taking his son with him. For a day or two there had only been silence from her, until the week before he was supposed to move and she'd informed him that taking Andres with him while he was starting a new job would be harmful for the child. And when he had protested? That had been when the not-so-subtle threats had started and he knew he had to do something drastic to convince his in-laws to let his son go or there was going to be an ugly trial. One that would have broken his wife's heart if she was still alive.

So, it was because of his love for his son and his respect for his wife's memory that he sat there waiting for someone he'd only known for a few weeks—and that had been mostly work related— to decide if she would be willing to help him convince his in-laws, and the courts, if necessary, that his son belonged with his father. Even if that father had made some mistakes before.

Realizing he had been staring into a cup of cold coffee, he glanced up and saw Lori at the cash register with her own cup. Laughing at something the man taking her money had said, she looked like she didn't have a care in the world.

But he'd seen those eyes as they had gazed at the little abandoned baby. She'd been beating herself up for not doing something to keep the mother from taking such a desperate action, though they both knew in the long run it was best for the baby.

Though wasn't that what he had thought he was doing when he'd left his own baby boy in his in-laws hands? Hopefully, the mother of the baby now known as Baby Girl Doe wouldn't have those regrets, though their two situations were nothing alike.

"Sorry, I was so backed up at the office after the delivery this afternoon and my last patient was a new mother-to-be with a lot of questions I needed to answer."

"No problem. I was behind too."

"Is there a problem? Is the baby doing okay?" she said, stopping across from him. The worry in her voice showing just how taken she was with the little abandoned baby.

"She's doing okay so far, but we're watching her closely."

She took a seat across from him, brushing

back the hair that had fallen into her eyes before lifting her cup and taking her first sip. She appeared tired with shadows below her eyes, but she still had a smile when she looked up at him.

Green, her eyes were green. He'd tried to remember the color of her eyes—it seemed like something you should know if you were engaged to someone—but all he could remember was the way they'd seemed to sparkle as the two of them had danced the night of the wedding. But these weren't just any green, Lori's eyes were the color of new grass as it broke through the dead brown grass that covered the yard after winter. The color that reminded you that the world would soon be awakening, it was the color of hope.

And that was exactly what he saw in her, the hope of a better future for him and his son. And if maybe he saw a little more, the hope that she might help heal the pain he'd felt since his wife had died, that was something he knew he needed to ignore. Friendship was something he was comfortable with. Anything more with Lori wasn't an option. She deserved to have a man love her like he had loved Katherine.

And that was a love he never wanted to feel again.

"Are you okay?" she asked, leaning over the table toward him. Had he missed something?

"Sorry," he said. "Long day topped off with a call from my mother-in-law."

"Is everything all right with your son?" she asked.

He could see the true concern she had for a little boy she'd never met. She was just that much of a caring person. What had all those exes of hers been thinking to let her get away?

"He's fine. I got to talk to him and listened to his jabbering for a few minutes. She 'invited' me to see my son this weekend. I told her I might be bringing someone for her to meet."

Lori went still, her eyes studying him as if she was trying to come to some type of conclusion.

He'd pushed too hard, too fast. "Don't worry, I didn't tell her anything definite. I'm not trying to pressure you into doing something you don't want to do."

She blinked and a very mischievous grin formed on her lips. "It's okay. I think I'd like to meet your in-laws. And I'd definitely like to meet Andres." The smile on her face relaxed into the more genuine one he was used to. "Fortunately, I'm off after clinic hours Friday so my weekend is free."

72   SINGLE DAD'S FAKE FIANCÉE

"So, you've decided to help me?" His whole body unwound for the first time since she'd told him she'd consider playing the part of his fiancée.

"Yes, but I need something from you in return. I spoke with DCS about the baby. They're aware the baby is preterm and is still on oxygen and nowhere near to being ready to be discharged. I know the case manager that's been assigned to the case, so I called her too. I told her of our suspicions about the mother's drug use. I told her I'd let her know as soon as we got the toxicology tests back. I also told her that I was interested in fostering and later adopting the baby."

Her words should have shocked him, and at some level they did, but he'd seen just how taken she was with the baby. And he'd seen the pain in her eyes when she'd had to pull her finger away from the baby's grasp. It was almost like the midwife and baby had formed a bond stronger in those few seconds then the mother had formed with the baby she had carried for nearly nine months.

"What did the case manager say?" he asked, hoping that if this was something Lori truly wanted the state would at least consider her.

"There is a lot of red tape, and there's an

application and a background check to begin with. I'll need to go through a training program and of course have a house inspection. And I'll need five letters of reference."

The list seemed daunting, but Lori had a positive nature and it showed as she went through the long list of requirements. "I'll be glad to give you a letter of recommendation. I would think as the baby's hospital provider it would carry some weight."

"I appreciate the offer, but I don't think that they'd take the letter from my fiancé. I think having a pediatrician that knows the baby being that fiancé might actually carry even more weight."

"You told them we were engaged?" Zach asked. Lori was definitely a woman who didn't waste time going for what she wanted.

She leaned over the table and laid her hands over his, then said quietly, "Yes. And don't look behind you, but it appears like we are about to have to tell someone else tonight before it gets out to anyone else."

She tightened her hands over his and leaned closer, "And please try to look a little happier at the news. Because if you don't take that shocked expression off your face no one is going to believe us."

74   SINGLE DAD'S FAKE FIANCÉE

He made his face relax and he pulled one of his hands away to cover both of hers and smiled. Far be it for him to mess things up now that she had put everything into motion.

His smile almost shattered when she looked above where he was seated and said, "Hi, Mom."

Lori had been running on empty for over four hours. The busy office, the delivery of the baby, and then being informed of the complicated process she would have to go through to be able to bring home Baby Girl Doe, a name that was wrong for so many reasons, had taken every bit of stamina she had stored up. All she wanted to do was have a few moments to make plans with Zach and head home to her bed. Telling her mother that she and Zach were engaged could have been left for tomorrow, except her mother was here now.

"I'm so glad you're here. You've met Zach."

"We met at the wedding. Jack introduced us." Her mother took a seat at the table, looking over at Zach, but he appeared as frozen as an ice statue sitting across from them. Was he even breathing? She knew that some men were afraid of their future mother-in-law, but this would never do.

She pulled her hand out from under his then entwined their fingers together, something that had her mother's eyebrows lifting. When his fingers tightened on hers, she felt a warmth inside herself, an awareness, that she wasn't faking. "Can you believe my mom's showing up right now? Right after I'd just said I needed to call her?"

With the squeeze of her fingers on his, he seemed to recover some. "Um, no. What great timing. And it's so nice to see you again."

"So what are you doing here?" Lori asked, hoping to give Zach a little more time to come to himself.

That was better. Now he just looked like a nervous man about to meet a future mother-in-law. And maybe that was the problem. Though they both knew this was just temporary, he'd been traumatized by his first mother-in law and what she was doing to him. It looked like she'd have to carry the brunt of this announcement.

"We had a meeting with the hospital board. You know they have a foundation that contributes to Legacy House. We were hoping that we could get some extra funding." Her mother stood and waved to where Lori could see her boss, though he was only her boss in a part-time capacity now that Jared had picked up most of the administration duties of the practice.

"Stop looking like I'm holding a gun to your head and start looking like you've suddenly fallen happily in love," Lori said to Zach when her mom stepped away to join Jack in the order line.

"I'm sorry, I just…it's your mother," he said.

"I know it's my mother. If anyone can sniff out something fishy going on, it's her. I'm going to let her know you've proposed. You need to help me convince her that we truly have fallen in love." Lori hated lying to her mother, but her mother would understand if she knew everything that was going on with Andres and she'd be thrilled if Lori was able to foster and someday adopt the little baby that had been born today.

"It's nice to run into the two of you," Jack said as he set down the tray that held his and her mother's drinks. "But shouldn't you both be off by now?"

"Lori had a complicated delivery and the baby has had some struggles," Zach said.

"We'd planned a date night, but it was too late by the time we finished," Lori said, turning toward Zach. "Isn't that right?"

"Oh, yeah, we've both been busy. Work and

all." Then as if a switch went off in his head, his body seemed to relax and his smile went fluorescent bright. "I plan to make up for it tomorrow night."

He looked so proud of himself that Lori wanted to kick him under the table, though kicking her mother or her boss by mistake wouldn't be a good idea. Instead, she beamed at him. Maybe her mother and Jack would put their reactions down to them just being foolishly in love, though she was beginning to think the two of them were foolish to think they were going to be able to convince anyone that they were serious about their relationship.

"You said you wanted to talk to me?" her mother said, looking suspiciously between the two of them.

Lori took in a breath, ready to spill out their announcement, when someone, she assumed it was Zach, really did kick her under the table.

"I'm so sorry, Ms. Mason. I really should have handled this different. I hope you'll forgive me for not getting your permission before I spoke with Lori." The sincerity on his face was enough to even convince Lori though she knew it was all an act. Where had his acting skills been a few minutes ago?

"My permission? Lori's certainly old enough

78 SINGLE DAD'S FAKE FIANCÉE

to decide who she wants to date," Lori's mom said, looking even more confused.

"I think possibly he had something else he wanted to ask permission for." Jack sat back looking at the three of them as if they were the entertainment for the evening.

"What Zach's saying, Mom, is that he should have spoken with you before he asked me to marry him."

"He asked you to marry him? But you…"

"And I said yes," Lori said, watching as the words stunned her mother. "I'm so happy. We both are."

"Yes, we are," Zach said, raising her hand to his mouth and pressing a kiss to it, causing an unexpected shiver to run down her body. "We hope you will be happy for us too."

When her mother found her words again, the questions, also known as an interrogation, began. Only the reassurance that they were planning to take their time to set a wedding date seemed to calm her mother. Surprisingly, Zach, who had been slow to begin with, managed to answer all her mother's questions. Lori would think he was a romance author the way he spun a story of the two of them being attracted to each other from the moment they met, but the time they had spent together at the wedding had only made those feelings grow stronger.

And when her mother had asked to see the ring, Zach had an answer for that too. He'd planned a night out with a trip to a jewelry store, but work had gotten in the way.

By the time Lori's mom had left the cafeteria with Jack, her mom might still have doubts about the two of them being ready for marriage, but Zach had charmed her enough that she was considering the possibility.

"Wow, that was a lot," Lori said, pushing back her chair so she could prop her feet up on one of the empty chairs. "I don't think we were prepared for that."

"I think we did pretty well," Zach said, looking very pleased with himself.

"You almost blew it the moment my mom walked up."

"I wasn't expecting your mom to show up in the hospital cafeteria. I still don't understand what she was talking about with Legacy House. I remember reading that new country music couple, The Carters donated a lot of money to the house."

"They did. And it helped cover the budget and some of the renovations that needed to be

80 SINGLE DAD'S FAKE FIANCÉE

done. But the house is having to turn down women weekly. They need to expand."

"Your mom and Dr. Warner are doing some great work there. Let me know if there's anything I can do to help."

"Oh, don't worry. As my fiancé, you'll find yourself volunteered for lots of projects."

"So we're really going to do this? And you're coming to Memphis with me this weekend?" Zach asked, still sounding as if he didn't believe her.

"I wouldn't miss it. I'm looking forward to meeting Andres," Lori said as they stood and cleared their table. "And his grandparents."

CHAPTER FIVE

THE NEXT MORNING, Zach texted Lori while she was getting ready for work to let her know that Baby Girl Doe had been started on morphine. Not that this was a surprise to either of them after both the mother and the baby's lab work had come back positive for multiple drugs. Though Lori wished there was something else she could do, all they could do now was watch the baby's neonatal abstinence score carefully and treat as needed.

Lori rushed through the rest of her morning routine so that she could stop by the NICU before going into the clinic. Because she was so early, only a couple of family members were visiting the unit. She looked for the baby she was already beginning to think of as her own, a dangerous thing she knew but one she couldn't stop. When that little baby girl had wrapped her hand around Lori's finger, she might as well have been wrapping it around her heart.

82 SINGLE DAD'S FAKE FIANCÉE

And now her heart had to think of that tiny baby she'd bonded with so fast having to go through the painful process of drug withdrawal. All she could do now was try to let the baby know that she wasn't going through that alone.

She immediately went to the back of the NICU to where the babies that needed to be isolated from the constant noise of the unit were located. Placed on the only warmer there was the label Baby Girl Doe, which for some reason bothered Lori more than it should. Every baby deserved to have a name even if it was a temporary one. She knew some of the nurses yesterday had been calling the baby Jane, because of her last name now being listed as Doe since the mother had never given them her whole name. Lori bent down over the sleeping infant and whispered, "Right now we'll call you Jane, but soon you'll have your own name. And it will be one that will let the world know just how special you are.

"How is she doing?" Lori asked when one of the NICU nurses joined her.

"She's doing okay. Still some tremors and her respirations are still too fast, but you know how this goes. It's going to get worse before it gets better."

"I know," Lori said. She'd seen these babies go through the tremors, high-pitched crying that couldn't be comforted, and even seizures. She wanted to touch the sleeping baby to reassure her that she was there, that she wouldn't be alone through it all, but she held herself back. It was better to let her rest when she could. "The case manager, Jessica, from DCS is coming today. Can you call me when she gets here, please?"

"Sure, I'll be going off soon, but I'll pass it off in my report." If the nurse thought it was an odd request, she didn't show it.

"Has Dr. Morales been in yet?" Lori asked.

"He stopped by here to check on Baby Jane, then he went to make rounds on the babies in the regular nursery."

Lori stood and watched the sleeping baby until her watch told her she'd be late for her first clinic appointment.

"I'll be back soon," she told Baby Jane, then reluctantly left the NICU.

She knew she was already getting too involved with the baby and if things didn't go the way she was hoping with DCS, she was setting herself up for a heart break like she had never experienced before. But what else could she do? It was like the decision to help Zach.

84 SINGLE DAD'S FAKE FIANCÉE

What else could she do but help him get his son back? Once her heart was involved, she had to do everything she could for the people she cared about. And all of this was happening so fast, giving her no time to protect herself.

She had immediately felt for Zach when he'd told her his story. Now getting to know him and realizing that she might go through the same pain, she was more determined than ever to help him.

She took the back way into the clinic and hurried to her office. She didn't think the senior Dr. Warner would say anything about her and Zach's announcement last night. Her mother was a different story. And with her working at Legacy House and sometimes escorting some of the younger pregnant mothers into the office, she knew a lot of the staff personally now.

But as the day went on, Lori relaxed. Tonight, she and Zach would plan out their story which was important if they wanted everyone to believe their engagement was real. Zach had managed to charm his way through her mom and Jack's questions the night before, but she had no doubt that his in-laws wouldn't be so easy on them.

She was just leaving the clinic to make

rounds and check on Baby Jane when her phone rang. "Sky, you're on your honeymoon. What are you doing calling me?"

"What are you doing getting engaged and not telling me?" Sky asked back.

"How did you find out when you're on an island in the Bahamas?"

"So, it's true?" Sky asked. Her friend's voice held all the disbelief Lori had expected. There had never been a man in Lori's life, at least not since they'd met, that Lori hadn't told Sky about.

Their volleying questions back and forth was getting them nowhere. Lori had to answer the question, even though she didn't want to lie to her best friend. "Yes, it's official. Zach and I are an item."

"An item I can believe. I saw the way the two of you were connecting at the wedding. But engaged? Isn't it a little early for that?"

"A lot of things have happened since you've been gone." How did those romance novels make it look so easy for the couples to fool everyone?

"So what, the two of you just suddenly fell in love and decided you needed to rush into an engagement?"

"It's an engagement, Sky. We haven't even

discussed a wedding date." Lori entered the back wing of the hospital and headed to the elevator. "Look, I can't talk right now. I'm making rounds and then I need to check on one of the babies in the nursery."

She started to tell her friend about Baby Jane, but she knew Sky would start worrying that Lori might be setting herself up for another disappointment.

"Don't think you're getting away that easy. When I get back this weekend we need to talk."

"I'm going to Memphis with Zach this weekend to meet some of his family. We'll talk when you come back to work next week. Have fun and don't worry about anything here. I've got this." The elevator door opened. "Got to go. Love you."

When her phone rang next, she was relieved to see that it was Zach. "What's up?"

"I just wanted to check and make sure we're still on for tonight," he said.

"Yeah, I was wondering if maybe I could just pick up some food and come over to your house." She didn't want to take a chance of her mom being home.

"If you're sure, that's fine with me. But let me order something. Do you like barbecue?"

"I love it." And that was just the kind of

thing the two of them needed to know about each other. "Have you ever done one of those speed dating things?"

"No, why?" Was that laughter in his voice?

"Well, I have, so don't even start making any jokes about it," she said.

"I wasn't," Zach said.

"Yes, you were. It really isn't as dumb an idea as you think. You can learn a lot about someone if you know the right questions to ask." The elevator doors opened and she headed to the OB hall.

"And why are we talking about this now?"

"Because tonight is going to be the most intense speed dating event ever. By the time we're finished, we should be able to answer all the questions your in-laws could possibly ask."

"Sounds like fun. I'll see you at six then?" Zach said.

Lori had hoped to spend some time in the NICU after she finished at the clinic, but tonight was the last night she had before the weekend that she wouldn't be covering deliveries. "I'm still waiting for the case manager from DCS. If I'm going to be late, I'll let you know. How's she doing?" She knew she didn't have to tell him who she was asking about.

"She's tolerating the morphine, but she's still

88 SINGLE DAD'S FAKE FIANCÉE

not eating well. She's getting IV fluids, but if she doesn't start eating soon, we might have to start tube feedings."

For the next hour, Lori rounded on the clinic's hospital patients. Answering questions and helping the new mothers as they were breastfeeding. She was ashamed to say that she had always felt a bit jealous of her patients as she waited and waited for the right person to come into her life to start a family with. And now she was giving up?

No. She wasn't giving up exactly, she was just taking some time off. Right now, her focus needed to be on getting approved to be a foster parent for Baby Jane. Besides, it wasn't like she would be doing any dating while she was playing fake fiancée for Zach. She'd be too busy keeping herself from falling for the handsome doctor to even think about another man.

It wasn't until she was headed back to the office to catch up with some of her charting before her next appointment that she finally received a call from the NICU that DCS was there to see Baby Jane. She started to text Zach, but this meeting wasn't a formal meeting.

It wasn't until she entered the NICU that a case of nerves hit her. She knew in her heart that she was the mother that Baby Jane needed. Now she just needed to convince the case manager.

"Hey, Jessica," Lori said, greeting the petite woman that was going over Baby Jane's chart.

"Lori, it's nice to see you. I have to say I was surprised when you called. I didn't know you were interested in foster caring."

"I hope you don't mind. I understand it's a little irregular to call the case manager directly. But this case is a little irregular too."

"You're right. We do see a few abandoned infants each year, but this was a little different with the mother delivering at the hospital and not giving any information, then leaving right after her delivery, abandoning the baby."

"I can't say we've had anything like it in here before," Lori said. She still wondered if there had been anything she could have said or done to keep Baby Jane's mother from leaving. There were so many things that could go bad after a delivery. The woman could have hemorrhaged to death after she'd left the hospital and they wouldn't know it. But all she could do now was hope for the best for the young woman. And give the baby she'd left behind the best life possible.

"I've talked to the nurses and it looks like with the prematurity and her Neonatal Absti-

90 SINGLE DAD'S FAKE FIANCÉE

nence Syndrome that she will most likely be spending several weeks here before she's ready to discharge. I understand that you have an interest in fostering her, and I'm sure you're aware of the complications and struggles you could face with this baby down the road. Her going through withdrawals could be just the start of a long ordeal."

As they discussed all the complications and challenges and the long-term effects of drug use in pregnancy, Lori became even more determined to apply to foster Baby Jane. She would need a strong mother and Lori was determined that she could provide the care and love she would need.

It wasn't until after the case manager left that Lori noticed that the nurses had taken a lot of interest in their conversation. When one of the nurses came up and hugged Lori and told her she knew that Lori would be the perfect person to care for the abandoned baby, Lori had to fight back tears. Bending down, she brushed the tiny bit of soft dark hair on Baby Jane's tiny head. Her eyes blinked open for a moment, and a grimace crossed her face before she wiggled her tiny body, then relaxed back into sleep. "That's right, little Janiah."

The baby's eyes blinked open again, this

DEANNE ANDERS   91

time remaining open for a few seconds squinting against the bright lights above her.

"Oh, do you like the name? I do too." Lori had always felt that the generic name of Baby Jane was wrong. Even though Janiah was a version of Jane, it was unique. And every child should have their own name, a unique name that fit them.

"It means God is gracious or gift from God. I hope you always feel that way. That you are a gift." Lori hoped that when this baby grew up and learned that her mother abandoned her, she would never feel unwanted. Instead, Lori hoped that she would know she was considered a precious gift that was loved from the day she was born. "Now, just relax and sleep. It's going to be okay. Someday soon you'll be coming home with me and I'm going to make sure that you have all the love that you deserve."

CHAPTER SIX

As Lori waited for Zach to come to the door, she caught herself worrying about the fact that she had chosen her comfiest and most worn jeans and an old volunteer's T-shirt to wear. It wasn't that she hadn't cared how she looked, she'd just used all her time on her computer searching for the most common questions asked at different speed dating events and she'd run out of time to do anything except grab a change of clothes and touch up her makeup.

Not that it should matter. It wasn't like Zach was interested in her, not that way. He had made no secret that he was still grieving over his wife. There was no reason to dress up for him. She was wearing what she would have been wearing when hanging out with friends. And that's what they were, just friends. Though, the fact that she had to keep reminding herself of that did worry her.

She pushed that thought away as soon as

Zach opened the door. It seemed there were many versions of Zach that she hadn't seen yet. This Zach, dressed in dark denim jeans and a navy blue fitted T-shirt was just another one. As her heart sped up and her breath caught, she decided that this one might be one that she liked a little too much.

That worrying thought returned. Never in her life had seeing one of her friends made her want to fan herself, nor had they ever made her feel like her heart had dropped to her toes.

"Hey, come in. I was just unloading the food," Zach said, totally unaware of the affect he was having on her right then.

She followed him to the kitchen without saying a word, afraid it would just come out in an embarrassing squeak.

"I didn't have a chance to ask what kind of barbecue you preferred, but I figured I was safe with pulled pork sandwiches."

She took a seat and a plate was placed in front of her. When she opened the foiled-wrapped sandwich, the tangy smell of sauce and smoked meat hit her. She took a bite, not even waiting for Zach to join her. With her mouth full she wouldn't have to worry about saying anything silly. With that first mouthful, she remembered that she hadn't had time to eat at all that day. That was the problem. It wasn't how delicious Zach looked tonight. It was just hunger pangs.

"This is good," she said, before taking another bite.

"I always thought Memphis had the best barbecue, but Nashville seems to hold its own with them," Zach said.

Then he picked up his napkin, bent over the counter and wiped the side of her mouth. For a moment they both froze. Zach's eyes had gone wide, as if he was surprised that he had been so bold, so intimate. There was suddenly an awkwardness that had never been between them before.

Unable to let the silence go on any longer, Lori took the napkin from his hand and wiped again at the spot where some sauce had dripped. "But is our BBQ messier than Memphis's?"

"It seems so," Zach said as he moved away from her. And though she could tell he was still bothered by his actions, his body relaxed back into his chair and he picked up his sandwich and began eating.

"See, these are the things we need to know about each other. We both like messy barbecue," Lori said, hoping to put Zach more at ease.

For the next few moments, they ate in silence, then cleaned everything up.

"Where do you want to do this?" she asked.

"Follow me," Zach said, leading her to a room off the side of the kitchen where there were deep cushy sofas, bookshelves and lots of toys. Toys for a little boy who had never gotten the chance to play here in the room his father had designed just for him.

She took a seat on one of the sofas and reached into her bag, pulling out a stack of papers she'd printed off one of the speed dating websites.

"What's that?" Zach asked as he took a seat on the sofa across from her.

"I printed out some questions to help us to get to know each other better." Reading over the papers, she found a question that she wanted to ask. "Like this one. What was your favorite game to play when you were a child?"

"Baseball," Zach answered.

"Okay, like, did you play in high school, college?"

"I played high school ball. I wasn't good enough to play college ball. Besides, I was busy with premed classes."

"Now we're getting somewhere. So, how old

were you when you decided you wanted to be a doctor?"

"I don't know. I guess when I was in high school. I took one of those tests they give you to help decide what your strengths are. How about you? When did you decide to become a midwife?"

"I worked labor and delivery when I got out of nursing school. There was a midwife there that I really admired. She had a way with her patients that made me want to be like her. So, I applied to midwifery school here in Nashville." She smiled. "Now you ask me another question."

She handed him a copy she'd made then waited as he read through some of the questions. And waited. And waited. "It's okay. Just pick one."

"I'm sorry, I just don't understand how knowing your favorite season is going to help us make people believe that we're in a relationship."

"Well, my favorite season is spring. That should tell you that I like new beginnings, which helps you understand something about my personality. If this was a real speed dating event and I asked you what your favorite season was and you answered that it was winter,

I might believe that the two of us wouldn't be a good match and move on to the next person."

"But there isn't anyone else to move on to and learning that I played baseball or that I also would pick spring as my favorite season is just superficial information. If you really want to know someone, I would think you'd need to ask more personal questions."

"Some of the questions are more personal. Just give it a chance." She was a little put out by his reaction to her plan for them to get to know each other, but she wasn't about to give up. She turned the page and asked the first question there. "What are your top three turn-ons?"

Her mouth fell open as Zach's eyes went wide. When he busted out laughing, she couldn't help but join him. "Are you telling me that two strangers sitting across a table from each other that have never met before ask those type of questions?"

It took a moment for Lori to answer as she was caught somewhere between the ridiculousness of the question and the fact she'd actually read it out loud. She had managed to embarrass herself at the same time as make herself laugh so hard that her stomach was beginning to hurt.

"I promise I've never asked a stranger that in my life," she said when she could finally get in enough oxygen to breath and talk at the same time. "I'm sorry. This isn't going anything like I had planned."

"Okay, so why don't we just throw these papers in the trash, and start over," Zach said as he reached for her copies of paper and left the room to dispose of them.

Zach was still laughing when he made it to the kitchen trash can. He hadn't laughed so hard in months. There was something about Lori that brought out a happiness that he had honestly thought he'd never feel again.

He saw a napkin lying in the trash can, reminding him of earlier when he'd reached up to wipe the sauce off Lori's face. It had been instinctual, but at the same time had seemed intimate. Too intimate for a man who'd just lost his wife a year before. Too intimate for a man who didn't ever want to feel the joy, and pain, of loving someone again. He'd crossed a line that he needed to keep between the two of them if they were going to go forward with their plan of a fake engagement. Maybe it was time he read one of those romance books with the fake fiancée to see just how the people in those books handled it.

He returned to the family room and handed Lori a glass of tea. "Sweet, very little ice."

"Thanks," she said. "I'm sorry if I messed this all up."

"You didn't. It's just…look, whatever your favorite movie is or your favorite color is isn't what's important right now. I mean, any of that stuff wouldn't really matter if we really had fallen in love as quickly as we want people to think we did. Wouldn't part of the fun of a new relationship be finding out about each other as we grew as a couple? Maybe, not knowing everything about each other is a good excuse for why we're not rushing into a wedding. We're taking our time. Enjoying this part of the relationship."

She smiled and nodded at him. "Okay. I give in. You're right. You don't need to know my favorite color or movie. Especially if you can remember things like how I like my tea. So, what do we need to know?"

"I think we did really good with your mother. We told her mostly the truth. We'd liked each other from the time we met, which is true for me. And we got better acquainted at the wedding."

"It was a little easier for her to believe be-

100 SINGLE DAD'S FAKE FIANCÉE

cause she thinks we slept with each other that night."

Zach choked on the swallow of tea he'd just taken. "What? Why would she think that?"

"She was at the house the morning after and caught me coming into the house with my bridesmaid dress still on. I told her I'd spent the night at your house. She assumed we had slept together and I didn't see any reason to deny it."

Zach wasn't sure what to say to that. No wonder the woman had been giving him the once-over. "That's not something I would ever do."

"Let my mom think that we'd slept together? I have to say she was pretty shocked."

"No. I wouldn't sleep with someone the first time I'd gone out with them. I have to know someone better than that." Which was one of many reasons he'd not slept with anyone since his wife had passed.

"I wouldn't do that either. I hadn't even slept with my last boyfriend and we'd dated for three months. Which was why my mother was shocked." The defensiveness in her voice was apparent.

"I didn't mean to suggest you would. And even if you did, I wouldn't judge you. And if you and your ex hadn't slept together by that time, it seems that one or both of you knew that you didn't belong together." He didn't like the fact that a part of him couldn't deny that he was glad that she hadn't slept with that jerk of an ex of hers. He hadn't even known her then. Had never even met her ex, but he had to be a jerk if he hadn't seen what he had in Lori. Couldn't the man see how amazing she was? She was beautiful and kind, and even Zach was feeling an attraction for the woman, though he knew the last thing he needed to do was to get involved with someone like Lori. Someone who'd want a man to give all of himself to her. Unfortunately, there wasn't a lot of Zach left after losing his wife.

So he told himself that it was just the protectiveness for a friend that he was feeling, but he knew it was more. It was jealousy and possessiveness which he had no right to feel. But it seemed no matter how many times he told himself that all he wanted was friendship, everything changed whenever he was around Lori. He could deny it all he wanted to, but his body was aware of her every time she was near. It was as if there was a magnetic pull between the two of them that kept inching him closer and closer to doing something totally irrational like kissing her, something that would surely lead to even more of a temptation that he wasn't ready for. Not now. Maybe not ever. Especially not when he knew that he would not only be betraying Katherine, but also he would be betraying the trust he was building between him and Lori.

She was helping him out, doing him a favor so big he would never be able to repay it. It would never be fair to ask her to give up on her search for that happily-ever-after that she so wanted for a man who could never promise to feel the love that he knew she deserved. And she'd just broken up with that Donald guy. No matter how much she might deny it, she was vulnerable now. He should be protecting her from any more pain. Instead, he was finding that he needed to protect her from him.

No, from now on he had to ignore even the smallest acts of touching her. Hadn't just brushing her mouth with his napkin stoked a burning desire inside his chest? He could try to blame it on the barbecue they'd been eating, but he knew better.

"Speaking of your ex, is this arrangement with me going to cause any problems for you? With your search for this Mr. Right you've been looking for?"

He found himself becoming more and more anxious when she didn't answer him right away.

"You know, I think I'm going to take some time off from that. Right now, I want to concentrate on my application to foster Janiah. Then there will be the two of us settling in to a routine together. It's not like I was getting any closer to finding what I was looking for. I'm not even sure what it is that I want anymore. Maybe for right now I just need to spend time with my friends." She smiled at him, a bright smile that dazzled him with the happiness it contained. "Besides, this fake fiancée act is kind of fun, even if our speed dating hasn't worked out like I planned. Any suggestions to fix that?"

With that statement, Zach let some of the guilt he was feeling go. Lori was enjoying herself, enjoying spending time with him as a friend. All he had to do was keep things between the boundaries of that friendship and things between them would work out okay.

"How about we just talk, like two people wanting to learn more about each other? The rest will follow. If we have questions that we can't answer, we just put it down to we're still learning about each other."

104 SINGLE DAD'S FAKE FIANCÉE

"There's one thing we do need to discuss before we meet your in-laws this weekend, but I'm afraid it's going to be painful."

"It's okay. I've admitted to you how I basically abandoned my son. What could be worse?"

"You didn't abandon, Andres. You love your son and you are doing everything you can to get him back without hurting your in-laws. What my father did was abandonment. He just took off and didn't look back. You would never do that. You're a good man, Zach. That's why I think your in-laws might think it's a little strange that you've never told me anything about your wife."

Zach took in a big breath, then let it out. He knew this was coming. At some point he'd have to tell Lori about Katherine. He just didn't know where to start.

And then he suddenly did. "You remember how you've talked about love at first sight?"

"Is that what happened?"

"Absolutely not. We were both in the premed program and to begin with we barely noticed each other. It started with a project for one of our classes and then there were the study groups we were both involved in. Before long, it seemed we were together all the time, either studying or going to concerts with our friends. We moved in together our last year of college." He could still remember their first place with its mix of his and hers furniture they'd assembled. They'd studied late and made love even later. "It wasn't until we'd both started to apply to medical school that we realized we might be living in not only separate homes, but possibly separate states. That's when we began talking about marriage."

"Did you have a big wedding?" Lori asked, her eyes full of so much genuine interest that he couldn't help but wonder if she was thinking of his and Katherine's romance like it was one of her romance books. If so, she was going to be very disappointed with the ending.

"No, not really. Just friends and family. We were both lucky enough to get into Emory, but between Atlanta's rent rates and our tuition, we were broke." They'd both had to take out loans while they were in school. "Those were years of hot dogs, noodles and too little sleep. But now, when I look back on them, I realize how precious they were. We grew together so much that year because all we really had was each other."

"It does seem that we don't appreciate the

things we have while we have them, doesn't it?" Lori said. "But then you had Andres."

"Yes, then we had Andres." It seemed like he'd been on an amazing ride for all the eight years of their marriage. They'd had good times. Hard times. Good times again. And then there had come the worst of times. "We had been so excited about having a baby. We'd barely gotten our practices off the ground, but neither of us wanted to wait any longer before we started a family.

"When Andres was born, we were both so happy. I never dreamed that in less than forty-eight hours she'd be gone." How could he have known? She'd looked so beautiful holding his son, her hair damp with sweat, her eyes bright with tears. The next few hours had been the happiest they'd ever had together.

And then she'd just been gone, taking all that love and happiness they'd shared with her. "She coded right before we were being released from the hospital. The autopsy showed that she'd had a blood clot. I still don't understand why. I guess I never will."

"I'm so sorry that things ended that way for the two of you," Lori said.

He saw her brush a tear from her own cheek and then realized for the first time that he'd been crying too. His story had started with so much hope and happiness, then ended so badly for both Katherine, him and her parents. "I didn't mean to make you cry."

"Don't apologize to me. I'm the one that made you go through all of that again," Lori said.

"You know, I think you're the first person I've ever spoken to about Katherine like this. Thank you for listening."

Later that night, when he watched Lori walk out to her car, he was still surprised by the fact that he'd been able to talk so openly about his marriage and the loss of his wife with her. He'd kept so much of his pain locked up inside him, yet it had seemed so easy to open up to Lori. While he still felt drained from talking so much about his marriage, he felt as if a weight had been lifted too. As if processing everything that had happened to the two of them had helped heal something inside him. He realized he'd been forced to remember the good times they'd had instead of just the end when he'd lost her. Was it possible that he was finally healing?

Looking around the home he'd worked to make for him and his son, he felt a new spark of hope.

108 SINGLE DAD'S FAKE FIANCÉE

And it was all because of Lori, a woman with a big heart that wanted to not only help him and his son, but also a tiny baby that lay in the nursery waiting for someone to claim her. He just had to make sure that when this was all over, that big heart of hers wasn't a shattered mess, like his own.

CHAPTER SEVEN

FOR THE REST of the week Lori and Zach communicated mainly with texts, with Lori covering the deliveries at night and Zach busy with the Well Baby nursery and the NICU. In between deliveries and clinic hours, Lori worked on her application for foster parenting and registered for the training classes starting the next week. They occasionally ran into each other on a delivery or in the nursery where Lori had begun to spend time between deliveries with Baby Jane. Lori knew that babies withdrawing from drugs could take weeks before they were weaned off their morphine drips, it seemed that the baby's abstinence score was slowly creeping up over the last couple days, requiring more medication to keep her tremors and respirations at a safe level. As Zach had feared, he'd had to order tube feedings on Baby Jane though the good news was that she was tolerating the feedings well.

110   SINGLE DAD'S FAKE FIANCÉE

By the time Lori climbed into Zach's car on Saturday morning to make the trip to Memphis, she was a nervous wreck. She'd spent the week either worrying about Janiah or worrying that she wasn't going to be able to help Zach as much as she hoped. What if Zach's in-laws took an instant dislike to her? While she wanted to make sure that they were aware that Zach wasn't alone, that there was someone beside him ready to fight for custody of his son, she was also hoping that things wouldn't come to that. She hoped that meeting her and seeing her and Zach together would ease them into thinking of Andres belonging with the two of them.

Zach handed her a soft velvet black box, dragging her from thoughts that were getting her nowhere. She stared at it then looked back at him. "What's this?"

"If we want my in-laws to take us seriously, I figured we better make it official with a ring," Zach said, never taking his eyes off the road. "I didn't know what you liked, so I hope it's okay."

Lori held the box like it was a bomb about to go off at any moment. She eased the box open and found a gold band with a large teardrop diamond surrounded by smaller diamonds. She shut the box, her hand beginning to tremble.

"What's wrong? If you don't like it, we can exchange it after this weekend." The nervousness she heard in Zach's voice matched hers.

"What if this is a mistake? What if I mess up and make things worse between you and your in-laws?" She opened the box again, then shut it quickly. Were they really going to do this? The sight of the ring made things seem more real now.

Zach pulled over into a fast-food parking lot. "If you don't want to go through with this, I'll understand. I can take you home right now and everything will be okay."

"Everything except your in-laws will give you an even harder time when you show up without me. They have to suspect that it's a woman you're bringing for them to meet. Besides, this was my idea."

"Which was a lot better idea than mine, to get you to marry me," he said.

"You're right. That wasn't a good idea. But is mine any better? At some point, the truth will come out."

"And by that time Andres will be living in Nashville with me," Zach ran his hand through his hair and looked back at her. "It's up to you.

112 SINGLE DAD'S FAKE FIANCÉE

I understand. It's hard to fake something like this."

She opened the box again. The ring was beautiful, but the feeling in her heart that secretly wished that this was real was not. But how could she admit to Zach that the feelings she was having for him were seeming less and less fake? That the more she got to know him, the more she wished that she had met Zach later. Much later, after he'd gotten custody of his son and really started the new life he planned, maybe then he'd be ready to move on with his life.

She remembered the way he'd looked when he'd told her about his wife, the smile he'd had when he'd talked about their first years together, then the tears he'd shed when he'd talked about losing Katherine. All his emotions for his wife were still so strong that Lori wasn't sure that Zach would ever be able to move on from those. And risking her heart for a man that didn't love her wasn't something she would ever be willing to do. She'd had her heart broken by a man when she'd only been a child, a man who should have protected her instead of abandoning her. She wasn't about to let that happen again.

Still, she couldn't help but stare at the ring

that was no more than a prop for their performance as if it was the most beautiful thing she'd ever seen. Taking the ring out of the box, she carefully slipped it on her finger. It slid on smoothly and fit perfectly.

She held her hand up and let the sunlight bounce off the facets of the diamonds as she admired the ring. For a moment she let herself daydream that the ring was really hers, that the romance they were going to pretend was real. Maybe it was because of all the romance books she'd read, but she'd always thought engagement rings held some kind of special magic. Or maybe it was the love that was supposed to go along with the ring that was the real magic. She couldn't help but wonder if she'd ever feel that magic.

Suddenly, unable to stand the sight of the ring any longer, she placed her hand down by her side and forced her eyes away from it. She needed to concentrate on what was really important instead of letting her mind be filled with dreams that might never come true. Right now, this wasn't about her.

This was about doing what was right for Zach and Andres, though she couldn't deny that her own history with her father made her want to help the two of them be together even more. It wasn't fair that a man who wanted to be with his child wasn't allowed to. Not when there were children that dreamed of having a father who didn't have one. And if it meant playing a part to help make that happen, then that was what she would do. "Okay, let's do this."

Traffic had lightened by the time they hit the interstate and in three hours they were pulling up outside a tidy brick home inside a quiet neighborhood.

When Zach took her left hand and she looked down at the ring that now sat there, her hand shook. Then she reminded herself of why she was doing this. There was a little boy in that house that deserved to be raised by a dad that loved him very much. Not that Lori was an expert on good dads. Hers surely hadn't deserved her or her mother. But Zach, he would be a great father. That she knew for sure.

It was only a moment after Zach rang the doorbell before the door opened. Lori wasn't sure exactly what she was expecting, but it wasn't the jolly-looking man that griped Zach's hand and welcomed them into the house.

"Lori, this is Butch Harrison, my father-in-law," Zach said. "Butch, this is Lori Mason."

Lori had noticed that Zach still referred to

his late wife's parents as his in-laws, a sign that he still respected the older couple even though they were at odds where his son was concerned.

"It's nice to meet you." Lori held her hand out to Butch, and instantly thought that in any other circumstance it would have been.

A squeal came from down the hallway and then a brown-haired toddler, wet and naked, came running into the room. Before Lori knew it, the child had darted behind her, clinging to her legs. After the toddler came a beautiful older woman. With silver hair, blue eyes and a flushed face, no doubt from chasing the toddler, Zach's mother-in-law looked just like any other grandmother who'd come to the end of their patience with a certain little boy would look. Then in front of her eyes, the woman who appeared to have fought a war, and lost, straightened her back and wiped away all signs of defeat. Her tired eyes went on alert as if readying for another battle.

"Oh, Zach, I wasn't expecting you so early," the woman said, before turning her eyes toward Lori.

Lori gave the woman her warmest smile, before glancing down at the toddler still hiding behind her, his wet body soaking through the dress pants she'd worn. "You must be Andres."

The little boy stared up at her, his brown eyes merry with mischief and his smile wide with two little teeth peeking out at her.

Lori reached out for the towel Andres's grandmother held, surprising the woman so much that she handed it to her.

"Oh, you don't need to do that," the woman said when both Lori and Zach bent down to dry Andres off. "I can do it."

When Andres saw that it was his father beside him, he let out a yelp, abandoning Lori as he tried to climb up his daddy's legs as Lori attempted to dry the wiggling toddler. In seconds the three of them were kneeling on the floor all of them laughing, the little boy not even acknowledging that she was a stranger.

But when Lori looked up, it was the expression on Andres's grandmother's face that killed her enjoyment of the moment. Lori had heard of looks that could kill and she had no doubt that if this woman's eyes could shoot daggers, Lori would be lying in a pool of blood right then. But she'd been prepared for this and she wasn't going to let this woman's attitude ruin Zach's moment with his son.

"Kelley, this is Lori, Zach's friend from

Nashville. Lori, this is my wife, Kelley," Butch said, the smile on his face reassuring Lori that, at least for now, she was safe. "Zach, why don't you go get Andres dressed while Kelley and I get to know Lori. We'll meet you in the family room."

It wasn't that she thought the woman would actually hurt her. Lori spent most of her time around mothers. She recognized a protective mama bear when she saw one. Andres was actually a very lucky boy to have all of these adults care so much for him. It was just too bad that at least one of the adults was putting their own needs ahead of his.

Zach looked up at Lori, soundlessly asking her if she would be okay. Lori nodded and smiled at him as he picked up his son, now wrapped securely in his towel. Lori stood and started to follow Butch, then saw something on Kelley's face that surprised her. Fear. It was then that Lori realized that the woman feared losing her grandson as much as Zach feared never getting his son back. Did Zach know this? Looking from the outside, it might be easier for her to see than for Zach with his history with his in-laws.

Lori followed Butch deeper into the house until they came to what looked like had once

SINGLE DAD'S FAKE FIANCÉE

been a formal living room with its floral straight-back sofa and loveseat. Only now the room was scattered with toys. A lot of toys. Too many, it seemed to her, but grandparents were known for that.

"Please, have a seat. Would you like something to drink? Coffee? Tea?" Butch asked her, still showing none of the signs of hostility she had expected.

"A cup of coffee, no milk or sugar, would be great," Lori said. Though she usually preferred tea, she felt the need for something stronger today. She needed to be ready for all the questions she knew were coming.

"So, I take it you and Zachary are coworkers?" Kelley asked as she took the seat beside her after Butch left the room.

"We work at the same hospital," Lori said, not answering the question directly. Kelley would know soon enough that Lori and Zach were more than coworkers.

At least that was true. They were more than just coworkers. They were friends. Good friends. More than good friends. They were... what exactly were they? She couldn't say she'd ever had a relationship with anyone quite like the one she had with Zach. There was an intimacy with sharing all of this with him that she'd never experienced before. She had trusted him more with her feelings and fears than she'd ever trusted anyone. Just admitting that should scare her.

But that wasn't what was important right now. Right now, she had to win this woman and her husband over any way she could and pointing out what a great father Zach was would be a good start.

"You have a lovely house," Lori said.

"Thank you," Kelley said. "We've tried to make it a home for Andres, and of course, Zach while he was here."

"Zach has told me how much he appreciates you helping with his son while he gets settled in Nashville."

When the woman didn't say anything, Lori continued. "I know he's anxious for you to see his new home. We'd love to have you come see it."

Before the woman could respond to the invitation, Andres ran into the room, followed by a laughing Zach.

"Aren't the two of them so cute?" Lori asked, nodding to where Zach and Andres had settled down to play with a wooden train set. Then Zach made a choo-choo sound for the engine he held and Andres copied him, and Lori's arms came up and crossed over her chest, covering a heart that she felt would explode from the joy of watching the two of them together. Mistakes had been made by both parties when it came to Andres, but anyone watching at this moment would see that the two of them belonged together.

"Being cute won't help him when he's got a toddler fighting to stay up after their bedtime," Kelley said, looking away from where the two Morales males were laughing as they made the train roll on the plastic track they had made.

Lori wanted to tell the woman that there were more important things then being on time for bedtime, but one look at the woman's pinched face told her she'd be wasting her breath. Talking to the woman would be like talking to one of those knightly armors of steel. There would be no getting through to her. Kelley had decided a long time ago that the best place for Andres was with them. Whether that was still true or not, she wasn't willing to consider any other possibilities. How Zach hadn't seen this, Lori didn't know. Unfortunately for Kelley, Lori was just as stubborn as she was.

Maybe it was because of her determination to claim Janiah as her own that Lori could see that there was no compromise in Kelley's mind. Now Lori just had to figure out what to do about that.

She was so busy trying to figure out a plan that she jolted when Butch leaned over her to hand her the coffee.

"Be careful, it's hot," he said, handing her the cup then taking a seat beside his wife. "I guess I should have asked Zach if he wanted something."

"He's fine." Lori said. She was willing to fight an army bigger than the two of them to keep them from interrupting Zach and his son right then.

For a few moments there was a silence between the three of them, the noises of the father and son playing the only sounds in the room. Then Lori lifted her cup and took a sip.

"What is that?" Kelley asked, her voice an octave higher than it had been before.

Lori looked down to where the woman was staring, where Lori's left hand held the saucer Butch had given her. And where a beautiful shiny diamond sparkled on Lori's finger.

"I…" Lori let herself stumble over the words. "We were going to tell you. Zach wanted to do it himself, but then there was a wet toddler running up to us. That just didn't seem the time for it. We're engaged."

Lori held out her hand to show off the ring to Kelley and Butch. "It's beautiful, isn't it?"

"It's lovely," Butch said. The man might have been surprised by the announcement, but his eyes lost none of the kindness, though she could see a few tears gathering.

Lori had known this would be hard for the couple. They'd lost their daughter and now their son-in-law was moving on with his life. Or as far as they were concerned, he was. But Lori was beginning to accept that as far as his late wife was concerned, Zach might never be ready to move on. For a moment the thought made her sad. For her because she felt that there might have been something between the two of them if things were different, but also for Zach, as living with only memories seemed to be a lonely way to live. Then she remembered that none of that mattered. Not now. Now it was time for her to sow some seeds to help Andres's grandparents to come to terms with the fact that Zach was planning on building a family with his son.

"I told him you would be happy for him. I know it had to have been hard for him losing his wife, and for you losing your daughter. But I told him that you would understand that he, and Andres of course, needed to continue with a life that Katherine, your daughter, would have wanted them to have." Lori said the words, somehow knowing that this was true. From everything Zach had told her about his wife, she would never want things for Andres, or Zach, to be like this.

She felt a bit of guilt when she looked at the couple. While Butch's face hadn't changed, making her think he had accepted that someday this would happen, Kelley sat up, her back ramrod straight, her eyes still fixed on the ring Lori wore as if she was trying to find some way to remove it.

"I'm happy for..." Butch said, before being interrupted by his wife.

"We will talk about this later," Kelley said. She stood, then shot the two of them a look daring them to stop her. "Right now, it's Andres's lunchtime."

Butch didn't say anything when his wife walked away, heading straight for Andres. They both watched her as she said something short, and Lori imagined sharp, before picking the little boy up and walking back toward the kitchen.

Lori watched as Andres turned toward his father, the longing to stay and play with Zach clear for her and Butch to see. But it was the

SINGLE DAD'S FAKE FIANCÉE

longing, and pain, in Zach's eyes that caused Lori to take a chance and speak quietly to Butch. "You know the two of those belong together, don't you? You know Katherine would have wanted her son to be with his father."

She waited for Butch to agree with her, to admit that he knew what he and Kelley were doing, keeping Andres from his father, was wrong. When he didn't say anything, Lori looked over at him to see him glance at Zach and then back over at her, before standing. He shook his head, whether to them or to himself, she didn't know.

How did he do this? Where did he find the patience to deal with his in-laws when it was plain to see that they were taking advantage of his feelings for them? That had to be the reason that he was putting up with the way they were treating him.

She felt the anger inside her begin to boil. Zach shouldn't have to deal with any of this. He deserved better than to be treated like this. He'd lost his wife, and now they wanted him to lose his son?

As Zach came to stand next to her, Lori watched Butch follow his wife out of the room. She knew that Zach's father-in-law wasn't happy about the situation between themselves and their son-in-law. When Zach opened his mouth, no doubt to ask what had happened, Lori just held up her left hand showing him the ring.

Whether it was because of the defeat that must have shown on her face, or whether Zach was feeling the same disappointment, Lori didn't know, but he took her hand and gave it a gentle squeeze. Looking down to where their hands were joined, she immediately felt better. This was just one battle. There were more to come.

And Lori understood that in the end they would be successful, because after what she'd just seen, she wouldn't stop fighting until the Morales family was back together, father and son, as it always should have been.

CHAPTER EIGHT

ZACH WATCHED AS his son stood at the top of the stairs of the porch with his in-laws, taking a piece of his heart with him, just as his son did every time Zach left him. Maybe that was part of the reason he spent most of his time feeling numb and hollow.

But that wasn't how he'd felt today. Today, with Lori beside him, he'd felt hope for the first time since he'd moved to Nashville.

He waited until the three of them went inside before driving away. He tried to ignore that he'd seen Andres turn around and look for him before the door had shut. It was so wrong. So wrong to be leaving his son once more. Only the fact that Lori sat beside him kept away the tears that usually fell when he left his son. He reminded himself that the two of them had a plan. One that they'd begun today.

Not much longer, he promised himself and his son.

It wouldn't be much longer till he would be taking his son home for good.

"I think that went well," he said as he headed to the hotel where he'd reserved rooms for the night.

"What?" Lori asked, staring at him like she didn't understand him.

She'd been quiet for the last couple hours that they'd spent at the park, though she'd seemed happy to play alone with Andres on the gym equipment. And she had joined in to help chase his son around the park when the little daredevil had decided he needed to climb on every surface available.

"I said, I thought things went pretty well today. Maybe not as well as I hoped, Kelley did seem very skeptical of our engagement, but thinking they'd just hand Andres over when I presented them with the idea of our new family coming together had probably not been too realistic."

"Realistic? Zach, do you really think it's okay for them to treat you this way?" Lori asked, the anger in her voice something that he had never heard before. "Maybe it's time you were more realistic about what is going on all around you. Maybe you need to open your eyes and see what's really happening."

128   SINGLE DAD'S FAKE FIANCÉE

"I don't know what you're talking about." Glancing over at her, he saw that she was really upset. At him? At his in-laws? He didn't know which, he only knew he didn't like it. Because while there was anger in her voice, there was also pain in her eyes.

"I can't believe that they wouldn't let us take Andres to the park by ourselves," Lori said, then continued before he could interrupt her. "He's your son. Your son. Not theirs. Yet when you told them we wanted to take Andres to the park, they insisted that they come with us."

He understood her anger now. He hadn't been happy either when Kelley had insisted that they tag along "in case Andres needed them" even after Lori had very sweetly questioned what the child could possibly need them for. He'd thought Kelley would have an aneurism when Lori had pointed out the fact that Andres would be as safe as possible surrounded by a doctor and a nurse. But he didn't need Lori to tell him that his in-laws were overbearing, well at least Kelley was. What did the woman think he was going to do, steal his own son? Not that the idea of running off with Andres hadn't crossed his mind many times. Many, many times. But was that really the right thing for his son? It would fracture the only family that his son knew. It was important to everyone involved that he did this right. The last thing he needed to do was anger his in-laws and have his son involved in a court case that would get ugly. He just needed to be a little more patient.

No, he had to handle this, if at all possible, without causing problems with Katherine's parents. It was what his wife would have wanted.

But Katherine never would have wanted you to get yourself into this mess. Katherine would have depended on you to take care of her son if something happened to her. But you didn't. You took the easy way out then. You can't take the easy way out this time. You can't hurt Katherine's parents.

"This is all my fault. I shouldn't have let things go this far." He kept his eyes on the road until he pulled into the hotel entrance.

But when he started to get out of the car, Lori grabbed his arm. "The only way that you are at fault is that you let them convince you over the last months that you aren't able to take care of Andres on your own. Maybe that's what they really believe. Or maybe they're just using this as a way to control you. They're playing on your guilt, Zach. Well, at least Kelley is. She's been doing it since Katherine, I bet. Didn't you

130 SINGLE DAD'S FAKE FIANCÉE

notice that every time you brought up moving into your new house and our making plans for Andres to join us there, she brought up something about Katherine. She thinks if she stalls enough, you'll move back in with them."

Yes, he'd caught the digs his mother-in-law had made about Katherine always wanting to raise a family in Memphis. And later, when she'd asked Lori if she'd be quitting work after they married, Kelley had gone on and on about how Katherine had dreamed about staying home with her children, though they both knew his wife had always planned to go back to work.

"I'm sorry. I know I shouldn't have said anything, but it makes me so angry to see them treat you this way. I know it has to hurt to have the people you trusted and loved try to manipulate you the way they do. I just wish there was something I could do about it."

"You are doing something. You're here with me. And you're supporting me. That means a lot to me."

She removed her arm, and they both got out of the car. He could still feel the tension in her as they walked to their rooms. Her anger being directed at his in-laws in defense of him felt strange. She was mad because she felt he had been wronged. He couldn't remember the last time someone had been this protective of him. His brother agreed that Andres belonged with Zach, but he was very open about the fact that he had warned Zach at the beginning against letting his in-laws take over Andres's care.

Stopping in front of Lori's room, he tried to find the words to make her understand how much he appreciated her defending him while explaining why she couldn't blame everything on Kelley and Butch.

"How about a drink in the lounge downstairs?" he asked. He knew they both were drained from the stress of the day. Kelley had insisted that they stay for dinner after they'd come back from the park, giving her more time to question Lori and his relationship. While they'd managed to keep their story together, it hadn't been easy.

For a moment she seemed to hesitate. Maybe she'd had enough of not only his in-laws, but of him too.

"Sure, but I want to wash up first. Meet you down there in an hour?" she finally said.

It would probably be best if they just went straight to bed, but he wasn't ready to face the lonely hotel room. And he wasn't ready to say good night to Lori. Even when she was

132 SINGLE DAD'S FAKE FIANCÉE

angry, she was easy to talk to, easy for him to relax around. She'd even managed to make him laugh a few times in the last week, something that he hadn't done much in the last year.

Lori saw Zach the moment she stepped into the room. He sat at a small table for two, a drink in his hand and his elbows resting on the table with what looked like the weight of the world on his shoulders. She watched as a waitress stopped by and he glanced up at her and smiled. But even across the room Lori could tell his heart wasn't in it.

She was responsible for that, or at least part of it. She'd been so angry at having to keep her mouth shut as she'd watched Kelley do everything she could to make Zach feel like an incapable parent. Couldn't the woman see how much Zach loved his son? Couldn't she see how much Andres loved his father? And all of her concerns about Zach being busy at work and Andres needing a full-time parent, those were all just excuses. Now with Lori in the picture, she had even fewer reasons for her concerns.

And Kelley knew it too, because Lori had seen the fear in her eyes when Andres had hugged both Zach and Lori before they'd left tonight. They'd shown Zach's in-laws the family they could offer Andres as they'd played together in the park. There had been times when Lori had even forgotten that they were supposed to be putting on a show for Kelley and Butch. Once, as the three of them had been running with the toddler, each one of them holding one of his hands, she'd looked over at Zach and seen him smiling at her with such joy that she'd thought her heart would explode from the pleasure of sharing that special moment with him.

And that was when she realized what she had done. For the first time that she could remember, she'd opened herself up totally to someone. The thought had her stumbling, almost causing the three of them to fall down. But when Zach had looked over at her, she had hid the fear she felt at the realization. For the rest of the day, she was careful not to lose herself in Zach's smile again.

Now, looking across the room at Zach, she couldn't deny that something had changed inside her. For years she'd been careful to protect her heart from others, only to have this man tear down all the walls she'd kept between her and the rest of the world. And that scared her more than she wanted to admit.

134 SINGLE DAD'S FAKE FIANCÉE

"Hey," Zach said, standing as she joined him. "I was starting to think you weren't coming."

"I'm sorry. I called to check on Janiah," Lori said. She was glad she had come and seen for herself the situation between Zach, his son and his in-laws. She understood so much more of what he was going through now. But she'd missed her daily visit in the NICU.

"Janiah?" he asked. "Baby Jane?"

"We couldn't keep calling her Baby Jane. It didn't feel right." She'd seen the worry in the nurses faces when she'd told them Janiah's new name. By now they all knew she was trying to foster the baby. That she was getting more and more involved when she had such a long way to go to get approved by DCS worried her too. But her heart couldn't stop caring for the baby that had been abandoned. The fact that Lori had been abandoned by her father and understood the pain that she still lived with only made her want to be there for Janiah more.

"Just be careful, Lori. The mother could still come back and claim her. I don't want to see you get hurt."

"She won't. Besides, she wouldn't get custody if she did. At least not right away. She'd have to complete a rehab program to even be considered for custody." She knew that there was always a possibility of someone coming forward to ask for Baby Jane. It would be something that would keep her awake until she could go through the adoption process.

The waitress Zach had been talking to earlier stopped and took Lori's order. Once she was gone, Lori changed the subject. "I wanted to apologize. I didn't have any business getting angry in the car. It wasn't meant to be at you."

"I know," Zach said, looking up from his drink, his dark eyes locking with her. "Thank you for being on my side. And thank you for standing up to Kelley. It's hard for me to call her out when she gets started. I spent years thinking of her as another mother, part of my and Katherine's family. I know you're right. I know I need to speak up. I just keep thinking if I'm patient I can get her to understand that I'm not moving back to Memphis and I'm certainly not moving back in with them like they hope."

He took a drink from his glass then looked back up at her. "I promise myself every time I make this trip that it will be the last one. But somehow, I end up letting her convince me that she's right. That Andres does need the consistency and security that she and Butch can provide him. That my not being able to be a full-time parent isn't what he needs."

136　SINGLE DAD'S FAKE FIANCÉE

"What makes a parent a full-time parent? Just because you have a job, and I'll admit that it's not always going to be easy being a single parent with a job whose hours can change at any time, doesn't mean that you aren't providing full-time care. Single parents everywhere in the world are working jobs and still making sure their children are taken care of."

"Katherine's parents were older when they had her. Their idea of full-time parenting doesn't seem to have changed over the years. Kelley was a stay-at-home mom."

"And that's just another excuse and guilty move she's using on you. Don't let her do it. We have to meet each objection your in-laws come up with, with a solution that lets them know that you are prepared in every way. It shouldn't be this way, we both know, but if you want to get your son without having to face them in court, it's what we have to do."

She looked up and saw Zach's eyes studying her. "What?"

"You make me believe we can do this. That soon, all this will be settled and Andres will be coming to Nashville."

"So how about we make that happen? How about we invite Kelley and Butch, with Andres of course, to stay with us for a weekend?

Let them see that they have no reason to worry about anything. That you have it all handled. Maybe they just need to see where their grandson will be to help them take that last step to letting him go. And they need to see that you are seriously not considering moving back with them. Let them see that you are putting down roots, not just with me, but with plans for Andres. Start interviewing candidates for a nanny or get things set up at a daycare so that when they show up, they see it's a done deal. I think once Andres is there with you and you show them you have everything set to take over as his 'full-time' father, they won't have a choice but to leave him with you. Not unless they really intend on taking this to the courts."

She waited while he considered her idea. It had come to her when she started thinking about everything she would need to do to prepare to bring Janiah home. Showing that she was serious about fostering and willing to do whatever was necessary could make a good impression with DCS.

"It sounds great, but I don't see them agreeing to it that easily," Zach said. "But what if I invite them to a party? It isn't something I usually celebrate, but I have a birthday at the end of the month. What if we used that excuse

138   SINGLE DAD'S FAKE FIANCÉE

to throw a party? They'd have a hard time declining if I explained that my brother would be there and I wanted Andres to spend time with his cousins. It would be hard for them to decline that after all Kelley's talk about the importance of family."

"I think that's a great idea. We'll tell them it's all my idea so they don't get suspicious, since you usually don't celebrate. And it will be another sign to them that you are ready to move on with your life.

"We'll need a few days to plan it. I have a lot to do with getting approved for fostering in between getting ready for work. And planning a party will take more time."

"Let's look at our schedules before we say anything to Kelley and Butch. I'm thinking maybe sending out official invitations might be good," Zach said.

"Sounds good," Lori said, then yawned. "And so does bed right now. I better go up."

"I'll go up with you," Zach said, then he stood and reached out a hand to Lori.

She stared at him, not sure what he meant. Surely, he didn't think they were going up to her room. She swallowed. The possibility was tempting.

After a moment, he seemed to understand

her hesitation. "What I meant to say was that I'll walk you up to your room."

She gave him her hand and he tucked it under his arm as they started back to their rooms. It was an old-fashioned gesture that made Lori's heart tighten for a moment. One that was so charming that she had to remind herself once again that the two of them were friends, just friends, no matter what they might be pretending to others.

But her heart told her that wasn't true. Somewhere she'd crossed the line between thinking of Zach as just a friend. Not because of their pretense, but because of who he was. Who she was when she was with him.

She'd looked for the perfect man for herself for years, but it hadn't been until she'd accepted that the person she was looking for didn't exist that she'd found Zach. He wasn't perfect, but she could now see that he was perfect for her.

Except he wasn't. Not really. Not when he'd made it plain that he'd had the perfect love once before and the pain of losing it had almost destroyed him.

"Thank you, again. You really don't have any reason to be helping me like this," Zach said, when they stopped in front of her room.

He released her hand, but instead of letting

it drop, she found herself moving closer and cupping his cheek. For a moment the world shifted, her pounding heart all she could hear. She wanted to tell him what she'd just discovered. Those feelings of friendship that she had for him were growing, into what exactly she didn't know. How could she when the way she felt around him was something she'd never felt before. Friendship? Love? She wasn't sure. But what she did know was that she'd do anything to make sure he got his son and went on to live the life he'd been dreaming of. Whether she would fit into that life, she didn't know.

Unable to help herself, she stood on her tiptoes and pressed a kiss to his cheek. "I'll always be happy to help you, Zach."

She should have stepped back then. She should have walked away and left things alone. But when his hand came up, brushing her hair behind her ear, she stepped forward instead of away; she stayed up on her tiptoes and replaced her lips with her hand, then pressed her mouth to his.

His lips were warm and firm. She felt his body stiffen against hers and she started to back away when his hands came around her waist bringing her closer. Closer, until her body fit into his as he took over the kiss and all thought left her mind as she melted into him.

A door slammed down the hall, breaking the spell that had held them together as Zach lifted his head from hers. It was the look of guilt that she saw in his eyes that told her all she needed to know. She had been right. Zach wasn't ready to move on from the loss of his wife. He might not ever be ready to do that. And she had to accept that right now. No matter what she felt for him, she wouldn't let that come between the two of them and their goal to get his son back.

Turning, she opened her hotel door, then shut it quickly behind her before he could see the tears that had already begun to fall.

CHAPTER NINE

LORI MANAGED TO get through the first part of her Monday while avoiding both Zach and Sky. She knew that she couldn't hide out in the office and exam rooms all day. Sky was liable to come in and start with her questions at any time, but if she timed her visit to the NICU and labor and delivery unit just right, maybe she wouldn't have to see Zach.

The trip home from Memphis had been awkward as they'd talked about plans for the party. It was her doing, she knew. What had she been thinking to kiss Zach like that? Could she have made it any more obvious that her feelings for him were changing?

The door to her office opened, and just like she had expected, Sky walked in. The new bride was glowing, her skin tanned from the time in the islands and her eyes bright with happiness, until she looked at Lori.

"No knock?" Lori asked, forcing a smile.

"And pretend I hadn't seen you just shut your door? You can't keep avoiding me. What's wrong? Who are you hiding from and why do you look so down when the last time we talked you claimed to be happily in love?" Sky asked.

"I am in love," Lori said, her smile feeling even more fake as she tried to relax her face. "How about you? Were the Bahamas amazing? You look wonderful."

"Yes, the Bahamas were amazing, but don't change the subject," Sky said as she took a seat across from Lori's desk. "I know you too well. There's something more to all this than you're telling me. Just a week or so ago you were whining over that loser, Donald. Then all of a sudden you are engaged and in love with Zach. To be honest, I can believe the engagement easier than I can believe that you're in love."

There was no keeping the shock of Sky's words off her face. "Why would you say that?"

"Because all the time I've known you, you've been looking for someone to marry. A husband. Not a lover."

"That's not true," Lori started, then stopped. Wasn't it? Hadn't Zach implied the same thing at the wedding before he'd asked her to marry him?

144 SINGLE DAD'S FAKE FIANCÉE

For a moment she didn't have words. She couldn't think past the realization that both Sky and Zach were right. She'd never trusted anyone enough to give her heart to them. And look at her now. She could deny it all she liked, but she was so close to falling for Zach even though she knew it would be the biggest mistake she'd ever made.

"I'm in so much trouble."

Lori started from the beginning, telling Sky about the conversation she and Zach had at the wedding, about his in-laws, his son. About how she'd come up with this great idea for playing the fake fiancée so that his in-laws would see that he was serious about settling down in Nashville and starting a new life instead of moving back to live with them in Memphis. Then she told her about the kiss, that soul-searching kiss that had changed everything between them. When she was done, Sky sat back in her seat and groaned.

"I know," Lori said, agreeing whole heartedly with her friend's interpretation of the mess she'd made. "I've made a mess of things, haven't I."

"Are you sure he's not just using you?" Sky asked.

"None of this is his fault, Sky. He's such a

great guy. He made a mistake when his wife died and he's been paying for it ever since. It was my idea to help him. We're friends, or at least that was all we were until my foolish lips decided to change things."

When Sky busted out laughing, Lori couldn't help but join her. She was so glad she'd decided to tell her friend the truth even if she knew Sky wouldn't approve. "So, what do I do now?"

"I can't tell you what to do, all I can say is that you need to be careful. You're already in this absurd fake relationship too deep. Are you sure that Zach doesn't have any feelings for you? Besides friendship, I mean. It sounded like that kiss wasn't one-sided. Is it possible that there could be more between the two of you? Because from what I'm hearing, and seeing on your face, you're falling for this guy."

Lori had rewound the moment they'd kissed over and over, savoring every minute. She hadn't imagined the moment Zach had wrapped his arms around her. And he'd kissed her back. If it hadn't been for the slamming door in the hallway, who knows what would have happened. But she also remembered that look of guilt in his eyes. Whether it was from feeling like he was betraying his late wife or whether it was because he didn't return any of Lori's feelings, she didn't know.

"He's made it clear that after losing his wife, he doesn't want another relationship. Not like that. No matter what you think, I know better than to fall for someone who doesn't have feelings for me." Such brave words when she knew she had been so close to taking that last leap when that hotel door had slammed.

"It sounds like he's still hurting, but that could change. He's already made some changes in his life, showing that he's starting to move on," Sky said.

Lori's phone rang and she took it out, expecting to see a call from the hospital, as she was on call. Instead, it was her mother's name that came up. She started to let it go to voicemail, her mother was probably just curious about her and Zach's trip to Memphis, but it was unusual for her mother to call during office hours. "Hi, Mom. What's up?"

Lori listened to her mom's frantic voice, her body going cold and numb, her brain racing in a thousand different directions. "It's okay. I'm okay. I'll be right over."

Lori stood, her hand dropping the phone onto her desk, then looked at Sky. "There's been a fire...at the house...at my house."

* * *

Lori stood by her mom, Sky at their side, as the firemen dragged their hoses back to their truck. It was gone. The house she'd called home for all of her life was gone.

"Our pictures..." her mom began as she wiped at her damp cheeks.

"Remember I scanned all of them into the computer last year and stored them online. I can have them printed out at any time." Lori added that to the list of things she needed to do, knowing her mom would feel better with at least something solid she could hold after all they'd lost. "And we have home insurance."

But it would never be the same. No matter if they rebuilt it to exactly match the small two-bedroom home Lori had grown up in, it wouldn't be the same.

"I'm just so glad you weren't home. When the neighbors called, I panicked. I couldn't remember what day it was." Her mother said.

Lori remembered the way her mother's voice had quivered, her tears clouding her words as she'd realized her daughter was safe at work.

She stepped back, letting another fireman get past them on the sidewalk. "We're fine, Mom. That's all that matters."

"I should have had the electrical work checked

148 SINGLE DAD'S FAKE FIANCÉE

last year when we had the work done at Legacy House. Our house is even older than that one. I just kept putting it off." Her mom put her arms around her daughter's waist. "I'll find a place for you at Legacy until we decide what to do."

Lori knew that the home for pregnant women was always full and needed more room that it had already. "Don't worry about it, Mom, I can find someplace to stay."

"She can stay with me and Jared," Sky said. Lori hadn't been able to talk her friend out of coming with her after she'd received the call, even though the office had been full with waiting patients.

"I appreciate the offer, but you and Jared are newlyweds. You don't need me around." And the last thing Lori wanted was to be around her two friends who were so much in love that sometimes they forgot that there were others present. Besides, she didn't need to be reminded any more than necessary of what she didn't have.

"She can stay with me," a voice said from behind her.

Turning, she saw Zach and the senior Dr. Warner had come up behind them. As her mother threw herself into Jack Warner's arms,

Lori just stood staring at Zach. "What are you doing here?"

"Jack called me and told me what had happened. I called in a favor and got the rest of the day off." Zach looked from her to the burnt-out shell of her home. "I'm so sorry, Lori."

Lori forced herself not to follow her mom's demonstration and throw herself into his arms. But when he put an arm across her shoulder, she couldn't help turning into him and letting all the tears she'd been holding on to for her mother's sake free.

Zach carried the last of the items they'd picked up at the store for Lori into the house. Though Sky had headed back to the office, he and Jack had waited while Lori and her mother had spoken with the fire inspector and then helped the two of them as they went through what was left of their home. It had only taken a few moments for all of them to realize that there wasn't much that could be saved. There had been a box of jewelry that had been partially intact in Maggie's room, but Lori's room had been a total loss, the only thing he'd seen her take was a small metal truck that she pulled out of the back of what had been her closet. Standing in that room had been devastating

150 SINGLE DAD'S FAKE FIANCÉE

for both of them. Lori had lost everything she had. And he didn't want to think about what would have happened if the fire had started a few hours later. The thought of Lori lying burnt in the husk of the bed that had been left had his stomach tied into knots. That loss would have been so much worse than the mere objects that had been lost to the fire. Lori would never have made it out of the house if it had started while she was sleeping.

Which just proved, once again, that he couldn't let himself get involved with her in anything other than friendship. Pulling back from her in that hotel hallway had been hard, but he'd had no choice. Lori deserved more than that friendship. She deserved to have a love like he'd shared with Katherine.

And he wasn't willing to take a chance of losing himself to the grief that had almost destroyed him from loving someone so much that you couldn't imagine living without them.

"Thank you," Lori said as she came down the stairs toward him. "I really didn't want to stay with Sky and Jared."

He remembered how she'd complained about always being the third wheel with her friends on the night of Sky and Jared's wedding. "I have plenty of room. I had the guest room furnished last week so you'll have your own space. Besides, wouldn't it look strange if you didn't stay with me after everything that's happened?"

She reached the bottom of the stairs and he saw the pain in her eyes at his words. "So that's the only reason you offered me a place to stay? So that it looks good?"

"No, that isn't it. I just…we're friends. I would do this for you no matter what," he said.

The look of pain in her eyes changed slightly, turning to disappointment. Friends. They were friends, he was sure of that. But after the kiss, something had shifted. For both of them, though he could never tell her that. The fact that he had wanted her, had felt the need a man should feel but one that had been absent in his life, didn't matter. Lori would want more than what he could give her. She deserved more.

"I appreciate it. I'll start looking for an apartment tomorrow. Right now, I'll take those and then I think I'll turn in."

She reached for the packages of generic clothing and toiletries she'd purchased at the local discount store. She gave him a ghost of a smile before turning away and starting up the stairs. His arms felt empty. He wanted to hold her as she cried out her pain as he had ear-

152   SINGLE DAD'S FAKE FIANCÉE

lier that day, but he knew he couldn't. So, he didn't stop her. He let her return to the room she picked from those upstairs. He understood her need to be alone after her loss. And with the click of her door shutting, he realized he too felt a loss. The loss of the easy friendship the two of them had shared before that kiss had changed everything. He'd lost his wife, and for the first couple months of his son's life he'd lost Andres while he grieved for his wife. Now he was losing that special bond he and Lori had made together. Sometimes he wondered, just how much loss could he be expected to survive?

CHAPTER TEN

BY THE NEXT morning Lori had put everything in perspective and come up with a plan. Yes, she'd lost everything she owned, but it could have been so much worse. Everything she owned could be replaced. Oh, she'd had mementos of her childhood that she would have liked to keep, favorite clothes that would be hard to replace and copies of her favorite romance books that she had collected over the years, but most everything else could be replaced.

She thought about the small metal truck she'd found and had hidden behind her back when her mother had come up to her. It was the last thing her father, Jim, had brought her from one of his trips. She'd hidden it away years ago, not wanting her mother to know that she still thought of those first years when they had been a family. Maybe that was the reminder she needed. Maybe she needed to ac-

154 SINGLE DAD'S FAKE FIANCÉE

cept that she wasn't meant to have that white picket fence family that she read about in her books. But was it really too much to ask for?

Sky had offered to help cover some of her appointments for the day and have the others be rescheduled, but Lori had refused. There was no reason for her to stay home and fret. Besides, she had received a text from Jessica, Janiah's case manager, asking to meet with her in the NICU department that morning.

Hoping to get out of the house before Zach was up, Lori dressed in the scrub top and pants she'd bought the night before and made her way down the stairs. She told herself she wasn't leaving early to avoid seeing Zach.

She shook her head and went back to the list she had begun before the sun had risen. She had more than just herself to think of; she had to find someplace safe and affordable for when Janiah was ready to be discharged. She'd filed the necessary application for foster care approval and was scheduled that week to start the classes that were required. It was only a matter of time before DCS requested a home visit. And as of yesterday, she actually could be considered homeless.

Not that it would have come to that. She could have rented a hotel room or stayed with friends, though definitely not Sky and Jared. But then Zach had offered his home to her, so she actually was staying with a friend. It wasn't his fault if she had hoped it had been more than friendship that had him offering her a place to stay. None of her feelings for him were his fault. He'd told her right up front that he didn't want to love anyone again.

Stop it. You can't keep thinking about Zach that way. He's your friend. Your best friend.

That thought cleared her mind. She had a best friend; Sky had been that person for years. The one she knew she could count on. The one that would listen to her problems and always consider her feelings. And didn't that sound just like what Zach was doing now? He'd been the one to point out that she'd been looking for a baby's daddy instead of someone to spend her life with. No one else had seen that, or at least had the nerve to be honest with her about that.

She smelled the bacon as she headed down the stairs. It reminded her of the first night she'd spent in Zach's home. Had it only been a little over a week? It seemed so much longer. Had she really only known Zach such a short time? Yet here she was, fighting feelings for a man that she shouldn't have. Feelings that had come on so fast. Too fast.

156 SINGLE DAD'S FAKE FIANCÉE

She waited at the bottom of the stairs, not knowing what to do. She'd planned to just slip out the door without seeing him. But now she wasn't sure what to do. It seemed so rude to leave without telling him, especially since that scent of bacon frying told her he was up.

"Ready for breakfast?" Zach asked from the kitchen door.

"Sorry, I really need to get to the hospital early so I have some time with Janiah before I go to the office."

"The nurses tell me you've been coming twice a day. It seems that our Baby Jane has taken a special liking to you too. The nurses say she eats better for you than she does for any of them," Zach said before turning back into the kitchen. "But if you have a minute, I'd like to talk to you about something."

Lori watched as Zach padded on bare feet into the kitchen. His movements were so graceful that it reminded her of a big sleek cat that had a mouse in its sights.

"What's up?" she asked as she followed him, then stopped at the door.

A large buffet ran along the wall that separated the kitchen from the dining room. On the corner of the buffet sat two picture frames. One was of Andres when he was younger, around six or seven months. Dressed in a pair of denim overalls, the little boy gave the person behind the camera a toothless grin. Beside it sat the picture of a beautiful woman, her hair and skin fair, her smile almost as wide as her son's. You could almost feel the love that the photographer had for his subjects. Somehow, Lori was sure it was Zach who had taken both pictures.

Lori glanced at the rest of the pictures on the buffet, and was surprised to find a stack of books. Romance books. Unable to help herself, she went over to the stack and picked them up. The first one had a picture of a cowboy, dressed in leathers and a Stetson hat on the front cover. She went through the rest of the books and saw that they all had one thing in common. They were all written around the fake fiancée trope.

She went back to the first one and skimmed the pages till she found a piece of paper marking a spot halfway through the book. He was actually reading it, a romance book. The thought of Zach staying up at night reading a romance book in bed made her smile. She could just picture it.

The smile left her face and she swallowed. Maybe thinking of Zach, stretched out in bed

158   SINGLE DAD'S FAKE FIANCÉE

with nothing but a sheet and a book was the last thing she needed to picture right now.

"Coming?" he called from the kitchen, totally unaware of where her lustful mind was at that time.

She took a seat at the island, then waited as he served up the slices of bacon and a helping of eggs to a plate, then put it in front of her.

Going back to the stove, he fixed himself a plate then took a seat opposite of her. Still, he didn't speak until he'd swallowed a forkful of eggs and washed it down with some of the orange juice he'd poured them. "I know this is a hard time for you. I just wanted to let you know that you can stay here as long as you need to."

"Thank you, but I promise to be out at least by the end of the week," she said. She forked the eggs then shoveled them into her mouth. The thought of the fire turned her stomach to stone and she had to make herself swallow.

"There's no hurry. I have the room. Why don't you give you and your mom time to think about things? Besides, doesn't it just seem like it would be normal for you to move in with your fiancée at a time like this?"

So they were back to appearances for their fake fiancée plan. She didn't like it; it was much easier staying there when she thought of it as something a friend would do, but he was right. It would seem strange if she was in such of a hurry to move out when as they were engaged she should be making plans to move in.

"I have to think of Janiah. What am I supposed to tell DCS when they ask to do a home visit?" She'd worried about that problem until she'd finally passed out last night.

"Bring them here. There's another room besides Andres's. The two share a Jack and Jill bathroom. I think it will be a couple more weeks, at least, before she's ready for discharge, but we can set a room up in there for her."

"I'll have to tell them what happened, but I think they'll understand as long as they know I can provide a place for her. Jessica knows we're 'engaged,' I had to tell her before one of the nurses told her, but I've made it plain that we haven't set a date. I'm not sure what will happen though if I'm living here. They might want to do some type of background check if I'm still here when Janiah gets discharged."

While it didn't hurt for DCS to know she was involved with the pediatrician that was caring for Janiah, she wasn't about to falsify any documents with listing Zach as part of the foster parenting application.

SINGLE DAD'S FAKE FIANCÉE

"I'm not worried. You know I'll be there to help you with Janiah. This—" he motioned between the two of them "—whole fake fiancée thing has complicated things for you. Let me help you.

"Besides, it's nice to have someone to cook for." He stood and took her empty plate to the sink. She was surprised to see that she had eaten everything while talking to him, though minutes ago she'd been barely able to get a bite down.

"So, you'll stay?" His offer was sincere and she really didn't want to get caught up in a lease until she and her mother heard from the insurance company and decided if they wanted to rebuild.

"I'll stay. Thank you." Staying here, sharing a home, would be another step into Zach's life, which seemed even more dangerous than playing at being involved, but it seemed right. She wondered if she should tell him about another one of the romance tropes, forced proximity. Would he run out and buy more books?

"I saw that you picked up some reading material," she said. She stood and walked over to the sink and began working on the dirty dishes.

She looked over to see the dark tone of

Zach's face turn red. "It's not something to be embarrassed about."

"I wanted to make sure I was doing this faking thing correctly," he said, coming over to take a dish from her.

As they finished the washing up, she decided it was better that she not mention anything else about the books. He was only half through the one book and she wasn't sure how he was going to feel about the ending, where the hero and heroine got their happily-everafter. Or how she was going to feel when she and Zach didn't, no matter how much she was starting to want to.

By Friday, the two of them had gotten into a routine. Though they were both busy, they managed to meet in the kitchen every morning for breakfast where they'd talk about their plans for the day. At night one of them usually picked something up for the two of them to share while they made plans for the party that they'd invited Zach's in-laws to.

It seemed like they were sharing everything in their lives, which was why when she walked into her office and found Zach waiting with Jessica for the meeting the case manager had requested, she was surprised.

162   SINGLE DAD'S FAKE FIANCÉE

"What's up?" Lori asked, as a knot began to form in her stomach. "Is something wrong with Janiah?"

"No. There are no changes since this morning. They increased her morphine over night, but we knew that might happen," Zach said as he stood. "Jessica asked to meet with me here."

His look said he didn't know why he'd been called there any more than she did. If the case manager had needed any information about the baby's care, she could have met with him in the NICU.

Lori walked over to her desk and sat. Was it possible that she had been turned down for fostering Janiah? Was that why Jessica had asked Zach to join them? To help Lori accept the news?

"I appreciate the two of you giving me your time. I have to say, I'm surprised that you still want to foster, Lori, especially with so much going on right now. I heard about the fire," said the case manager.

The fire. Lori hadn't even thought about the nurses in the NICU department talking about the fire in front of Jessica, though she certainly should have. She'd been so busy that she hadn't even thought about talking to Jessica about it. But it made sense that the case manager would need to know if she was responsible for a baby that would need foster care at discharge—she'd have to know that the foster parent still had a home for them.

"I'm sorry, I should have told you. As far as the fire is concerned, I'll have a place to bring Baby Jane home to when she gets discharged. But can I ask you a question? Why did you invite Dr. Morales to this meeting?"

"I was told today that you two were living together and you had told me that the two of you are engaged. I don't know your plans, but I thought he might want to be added to the application process." Jessica looked over where Zach sat beside her. "Was I wrong?"

Lori didn't know what to say. She could see where the information she had to have overheard in the NICU would have made her think that Zach would be more involved with Lori fostering Janiah, but hadn't she made it clear when she'd first spoken to Jessica that she was doing this as a single parent? "At this time, I'm applying by myself, as a single foster parent."

"I'm so sorry. I just assumed if the two of you were planning to get married and now living together..." The woman trailed off, looking confusedly between the two of them.

"Does it make a difference?" Zach asked.

164 SINGLE DAD'S FAKE FIANCÉE

"I mean, anyone can see by Lori's application and by the time she has spent with the baby that she's the right person for Baby Jane. She's a midwife with a good reputation. She's caring and generous. You have to know that she'll provide a good, safe home. I've seen her with my son. She's great. Any child would be glad to have her as a foster parent."

His phone rang and he pulled it out. Lori could tell by the questions that he asked that it was the hospital. When he looked up at her, his eyes filled with worry, she knew that it had something to do with Janiah.

"Increase the morphine and start the clonidine, per protocol. I'll be right there," Zach said as he stood and headed for the door. Lori followed him out the door, Jessica behind her.

"What happened?" Lori asked as she caught up with him.

"She had a seizure. Not a grand mal, but still…" he trailed off as they exited the building and headed to the path that led to the hospital.

By the time they got to the NICU, Lori was out of breath from trying to keep pace with Zach. She and Jessica stood to the side while he examined Janiah, listening to her lungs and heartbeat. The seizure had ended and when Lori checked the monitors, they showed that the baby's vital signs were stable, her respiratory rate within normal limits. Whether this was because of the morphine being increased, the sedation relaxing the baby to sleep or the results of the seizure's effect on the baby's body, Lori didn't know.

"Is she going to be okay?" Jessica asked from beside her. "I know this is common, but it seems it would have happened earlier."

"With her being premature and her mother positive for amphetamines and benzos, it's made her care different than most cases. Zach was aware of that and has had the nurses watching her carefully. The fact that they've had to increase the morphine on a regular basis wasn't a good sign. This is a setback, but I know she's in good hands with Zach and these nurses."

"He seems to be very good at this," Jessica said as they both stood back and watched as Zach gave more instructions to the nurses. "I have to admit, I still don't understand why he isn't applying to be a foster parent with you."

"We've only been—" Lori hesitated, not sure what to say without giving the case manager the wrong idea about the two of them "—together, for a few weeks. Our relationship is so new that we want to take things slow for now.

166 SINGLE DAD'S FAKE FIANCÉE

Zach knows I'm committed to fostering Janiah, and I want to look into the possibility of adopting her too. He's supportive of both."

The expression on Jessica's face told her that the case manager still didn't understand everything that was going on between Lori and Zach. But then Lori was just as confused on that matter. Sometimes, when they were alone at night, discussing their day and planning his party, Zach would smile at her with something in his eyes that looked like more than just friendship. And when they parted for the night, there was always this awkward feeling between the two of them, a feeling that if just one of them made a move, the two of them wouldn't be going to bed alone that night. The night before, she'd almost done it, made that move that would change everything between them.

But when she'd gotten to the bottom of the stairs, she'd lost her nerve and instead had headed for her room with only a murmured "Good night" before almost sprinting to her door.

"But you are living with him. You consider his home your home right now?" Jessica asked.

"I do," she said. Coming to Zach's house at night felt just like coming home. Knowing he was waiting for her had her rushing there every night she had off. She knew she shouldn't let herself feel that way. She was only setting herself up for heartache once Zach had his son back with him and she had to move on.

"Okay, then. I think we can put in the application that you have a permanent residence with Dr. Morales and that will cover the living arrangements. There will still have to be a home visit. And because he lives there, we'll have to do a background check on him too. Of course, I'm not worried about either of those things, but they are necessary."

Lori tried to listen as the case manager made arrangements to meet with Lori for the home visit, but her eyes kept watch over Janiah as she slept.

CHAPTER ELEVEN

FOR THE REST of the day, Lori went about her day seeing patients in the clinic, reminding herself that Janiah was in good hands with Zach and the nurses. She'd made them all promise to call her if there were any changes, so when her phone rang, she almost dropped the phone in her panic before she realized it was the labor and delivery department calling.

Becky English was finally in labor after going a week over her due date. It was the fourth child that Lori would deliver with Becky and Will, two girls and a boy, and today another boy. Becky had told her that being an only child, she'd always dreamed of having multiple children so that they'd have someone to play with and grow up with. Her husband, Will, had been one of three, telling his wife all kinds of horror stories of what three boys could do to each other, but Becky had stood firm. She'd wanted four and now she would have them. From the smile on Will's face, Lori knew that Will was just as excited as his wife to meet their new little one.

"You're almost eight centimeters and the baby's moving down nicely. I know you went fast with your last one, so I don't think it will be much longer. I'm going to step out for few minutes to call the office to let them know I've got a delivery and then I'll be back."

She left the room, as the nurse and Becky's husband, Will, began coaching her through the next contraction and was surprised to find Zach waiting outside the room.

"Did something else happen?" Lori asked, her heart skipping a beat with the panic she felt.

"No, there've been no changes. I think starting the clonidine is helping and the nurses are keeping her from as much stimuli as possible. I just wanted to hear what Jessica said. I'm afraid I shouldn't have let her know that her handling of this, the way she acted like you needed me on your application, made me angry. Did I cause any problems for you?" He leaned against the wall outside Becky's room, his posture telling her that he'd had a tiring day. "Is the engagement going to cause problems for your fostering Janiah?"

170 SINGLE DAD'S FAKE FIANCÉE

She loved how concerned he was for her and also the way he had begun to refer to the little abandoned baby with a real name. "I don't think so. I told her to consider your home as mine, but I think it makes it even more important now that we get Andres away from your in-laws soon so we can stop this pretend relationship."

Zach pushed away from the wall, his body so close to hers now that they almost touched. And there it was again. That look he gave her, was that what people called yearning? The way his eyes locked onto hers like they wanted something from her. But what? She held her breath. Waiting for him to say something, to do something.

And then he looked away, and it was gone. "Let's talk about it tonight at home."

She wanted to stop him, ask him what it was that he'd been thinking, been feeling. But what if she'd imagined it all?

So instead, she nodded her head, then turned and headed to the nurse's station to make her call. Right now, she needed to concentrate on her patient.

An hour later, she was happily handing a little baby boy, kicking his feet and screaming loud enough to be heard down then hall, to his proud parents. "I think he's bigger than the last one. He's certainly louder."

She finished her work and helped the nurses get both mama and baby comfortable. And when Becky and Will asked one of the nurses to get a picture of them with Lori, she smiled and obliged them. But when they showed her the picture, and she took in the look of such love on the two parents' faces, the way Will was smiling down at his wife and new son, it tugged at that empty spot in her chest that always seemed to appear whenever she saw a father and their child together. Had her father looked at her that way when she was born? If so, what had happened that had changed things?

She had memories of her father, them chasing fireflies together on summer nights, playing card games together until it was time for bed, crying after he'd hugged her bye before climbing into his big truck and leaving. Then the memories became farther and farther apart, as her father began missing birthdays and holidays. Until one day he'd driven off and never returned.

At first, she'd cried and blamed herself. Then she'd gotten angry at him, swearing that she never wanted to see him again. Later, with her mother's help she'd come to understand that the anger wasn't good for her so she'd pushed back her memories of him and pretended he didn't exist. Until times like this, when they crept back into her mind and just wouldn't go away.

Zach was headed out of the hospital for the day, when an arm caught his. Turning he saw Dr. Jack Warner standing beside him.

"Zach, I'm glad I caught you," the older man said, his smile looking somewhat embarrassed. "I was hoping you had a moment to talk."

From what Zach had been told, Jack had partially retired months ago and had stopped doing deliveries all together, so it had to be something personal he wanted to discuss and not a patient. As the only thing the two of them had in common was Lori, he looked around for someplace quiet they could talk. "Sure. How about I buy you a cup of coffee?"

Turning around, they headed toward the café while Jack asked him the usual questions about his work and how he liked Nashville. It wasn't until they'd both gotten their drinks and found a table away from everyone else, that Jack finally got around to the reason he wanted to talk to him.

"You know I'm dating Lori's mother," the older man said. "And she's worried about this engagement that it seems you and Lori have rushed into. With the fire, and that stress, I'm worried about her. I've been trying to reassure her that you two know what you're doing, but she asked me to talk to you. I've reminded her that you're grown adults. Smart. Responsible. And I know the two of you aren't planning to wed anytime soon, right?"

Zach nodded his head, not knowing what to say to the man. What did he want? For Zach to announce his undying love for Lori?

Undying love? It sounded so wonderful until you were stuck living with that love all by yourself. When the person you had proclaimed that undying love for was gone. What were you supposed to do with that love then? Hadn't Lori told him that Jack had lost his wife? But here the man was, worried enough about another woman that he was willing to question another colleague just to put that woman's fear at rest. "Everybody tells you that you have to move on after you lose someone you love, but no one tells you how. How did you do it?"

Jack sat back and stared at him, Jack's thick gray eyebrows drawing together in a straight line. Zach felt the heat of that stare as if he was

174 SINGLE DAD'S FAKE FIANCÉE

being studied under a microscope and he knew the man was seeing right straight through to that part of him that had been destroyed when he'd watched Katherine take her last breath.

"I don't know that you really ever do move on," Jack said, picking up his drink, his eyes finally leaving Zach. "No. That's not right. Let me say that differently. You do move on, you have to at some point. But moving on with your life, doesn't mean that you forget. You still have your memories. You still have the love you felt for that person. You don't move on without those. You'll carry that with you no matter where you go, because it's part of you."

"But if you take all that with you, are you really moving on? Like you said, you still love that person."

"Just because you lost someone you loved, that doesn't mean you can't love again. The heart is an amazing thing, a remarkable organ that provides us with life. But the heart which we use to love with is bigger than what you see in an X-ray or CT. It can hold more inside it than any cardiac function test can measure. The human heart we refer to when we love someone just gets bigger and bigger, as big as it needs to be. It's not limited. It expands to love our children, each time one is born. It doesn't replace the love you felt for one child with the love of another one. It can love both."

It was Zach's turn to stare at the man. He knew what Jack was trying to tell him. He could still love Katherine while loving someone else. It didn't have to be one or the other. And Zach could see that was how Jack felt about his late wife and Maggie. Jack still loved the wife he'd lost, but he had enough love for Maggie too.

But that was never how Zach had thought. From the moment he'd lost Katherine, he'd believed he'd never love again.

And then he met Lori. Sweet, kind Lori, who had done so much for him, the only woman he'd met since the death of his wife who'd tempted him into wanting more than friendship with a woman. But how did he know if he had enough love for someone else?

He remembered the way Kelley had pushed at him with memories of her daughter, over and over again as if she was trying to compare Katherine to Lori when it was plain to see that they were two different people.

Even the attraction he felt for Lori was different from what he had felt for Katherine. While he and Katherine had slowly moved from friends to lovers, enjoying each step as it came, the need he felt for Lori was different. When they'd been standing in the L and D hall together earlier that day, desire had flared up inside him so fast that it had almost overwhelmed him with the need to touch her, to hold her, to feel the warmth of her body against his own. It was only the fact that they were in a hospital hallway that had kept him from pulling her into his arms and kissing her, a realization that had had him rushing out of the unit as fast as he could. It was only when he got back to NICU that he realized the guilt he'd expected to come, didn't. And that bothered him almost as much as his need for Lori.

He and Jack finished their coffee, the older man letting him absorb everything he said. When Zach stood to leave, Jack finally spoke. "I know you care about Lori. I think you care more than you realize, or at least more than you are ready to admit. But if you can't love her like she deserves, you need to tell her before it's too late. She was abandoned once. I don't want to see that done to her again."

Lori was still thinking about the delivery she'd done and the picture-perfect family Becky and Will had made when she got home that night. Zach had messaged her earlier that he would order out for them so she wasn't surprised to see a pizza delivery car pulling out of the drive when she arrived. She followed the smell to the kitchen and found Zach staring out the window.

"Is everything okay?" she asked.

Zach looked up at her, as if he'd just noticed she'd come into the room. "I'm sorry. What did you ask?"

"You seemed far away right then. I just wanted to ask if everything was okay. Did your in-laws call?" Lori wouldn't put it past them to cancel coming to the party at the last minute.

"No, I called earlier today and talked to Andres. Butch assured me that they were planning to make the party. He actually sounded as if he was looking forward to it."

They didn't talk again until they'd gathered the paper plates and napkins and taken what now seemed like their designated spots around the coffee table in the family room that Zach brought up the subject of the case manager.

"Jessica called me after I saw you in Labor and Delivery," he said. "She wanted an update on Janiah and to let me know that they'd have to do a background check since we are living together."

"I meant to tell you about that tonight. I hope

178 SINGLE DAD'S FAKE FIANCÉE

it's not a problem. I think you just have to sign a form agreeing to it."

"It's fine. Not a problem," Zach said, handing her a plate and opening the pizza box.

She took a piece and put it on her plate, not bothering to take a bite.

"What's wrong?" Zach asked. "If it's Janiah, I checked on her a few minutes before you got here. There've been no more seizures."

"I stopped by to see her before I left the hospital." And then she'd stood there for half an hour before she could force herself to leave. "Am I doing the right thing? Pushing to foster Janiah and to adopt her? Or am I being selfish?"

"Why would you ask that? You already love that baby. You've done a lot of work to get qualified for fostering. What happened to make you think that baby wouldn't be lucky to have you as a mother?"

"I'm just worried that maybe she needs more than me. I grew up without a father. Do I want that for her?" Lori felt so confused. Yes, she'd grown up without a father, but she'd still had a good childhood. A happy one for the most part. Maybe it was because she'd had a father for a few years that she had missed that when it was gone.

"I'm going to be single father to Andres. I know he'll miss having a mother, but there's nothing I can do about that. All I can do is love him."

Lori knew he was right. Lori was willing to love Janiah twice as much if necessary. And Zach was going to be a great father. Saying that Janiah would be better with someone else was like agreeing with Kelley that Andres needed both her and Butch to care for him. "You're right. I will love Janiah and give her the best life possible."

"We both know there could be complications with any baby born to a mother who tested positive for drugs. I've ordered a CT. It will tell us if there is anything besides the withdrawal that caused the seizure. Without having any history on the mom, it's hard for us to know what else to look for. There's no sign of infection. We can rule that out. But there's a possibility that there could have been some fetal distress during labor that we couldn't be aware of. If so, there could be some permanent damage to the brain. You need to be prepared for that."

Lori had already considered that possibility. It didn't change a thing about her wanting to adopt Janiah. It scared her, but it didn't change her mind. "I am."

"I knew you would be. It's why I think you will be a great mother for her. She needs someone that's prepared to love her no matter what," Zach said. He took a swallow from his glass of wine.

"And as far as Janiah needing two parents, there's always my invitation to marry you." He smiled, letting her know that he was joking.

She understood that he wasn't serious. He had come a long way in the past weeks from being the man who thought he had to have a wife to raise his son. Not that it had been because of her. Not really. She'd just been the one to point out the mind games his mother-in-law had been playing with him. He'd just needed to get over his guilt of leaving his son's care to his in-laws at the beginning. She knew he had accepted now that though he might have made the wrong decision then, he was doing the right thing now for his son.

But what if he was serious? Would you take his offer now? Could you live with him as his wife, raise children with him, knowing that he didn't love you? That he couldn't love another woman after losing his wife?

She refused to answer the questions that flooded her mind. Better to change the subject than dwell on things she had no answer for. "So, tell me about the nanny that's coming to interview."

They discussed the applicants he'd spoken with over the phone, and the one he'd chosen to interview in person, then moved on to the arrangements he'd made with the caters for the party.

They finished half the bottle of wine, and cleaned up the leftovers of their dinner before they headed up the stairs to bed. Once more there was that awkward point where the two of them would go to their separate rooms. Once more she saw that longing, that hunger, in Zach's eyes when he told her good night, then hesitated before he turned toward his room.

She stood there watching him leave her, hoping that he'd turn around and reach out a hand toward her. When his door shut, she let out a breath she didn't realize she was holding. It would be another night she'd sleep alone. Another night that the two of them could share, if just one of them had the courage to take that step.

She walked toward his door, lifting her hand to knock, then stopped. What if she had read that longing look in his eyes wrong? What would it do to their friendship, the only thing he'd said he could offer her, if she slept with him? And how would she ever walk away from him if she allowed them to get any closer?

It was already a painful edge she walked between their friendship and the feelings that were growing between them. Painful because she knew if she ever let down her guard and allowed herself to love Zach, all that waited for her would be the heartbreak of knowing he could never feel the same for her.

Slowly, she dropped her hand, then walked away.

CHAPTER TWELVE

"You know, it feels really strange to be blowing up balloons for your own birthday party," Zach said, attaching a string to another yellow balloon before tying it to the other ones he'd been working on. He'd insisted that he'd grown out of the age for wanting balloons, but Lori had reminded him that Andres would love them.

"Stranger than throwing yourself a party?" Lori asked as she worked to tie two balloons together, reaching for one of them as it floated from her hand.

Zach grabbed the string, pulling the balloon down right before it joined its friends that were huddled on the ceiling. "At this rate there will be more up there than on the chairs."

"Less talking, more blowing," Lori teased, a smile cracking open a face that had been way too serious the last few days.

The doorbell rang and they looked at each other. They'd both come home early to finish

184 SINGLE DAD'S FAKE FIANCÉE

the decorating and all their supplies had been delivered earlier in the week except for what the caterer was bringing them the next day.

"Maybe it's an early birthday present," Lori said as they went to the door.

But when Zach opened the door, the surprise was much more than a birthday gift. Standing on the porch stood his in-laws with Butch holding Andres, who was fast asleep and draped across his shoulder.

"This is a surprise," Zach said. "I wasn't expecting you till tomorrow."

"We decided it would be best to drive down early," Butch said. The sour look on Kelley's face said she didn't want to be there at all. "You never know what could happen in the morning and we didn't want to miss this party. Where can I take him?"

Zach was so surprised that for a moment he just stood in the doorway.

"His room is up the stairs on the right," Lori said, pulling on Zach's arm so that he stepped out of the way.

As Butch and Kelley came in the room, Zach realized that this was really happening. Andres was here, in the home Zach had made for the two of them. "I'll take him."

Zach reached over and took his sleeping son from Butch, the weight and warmth of the toddler turning his heart into a gooey mess. He was home. Andres was finally at home.

He looked over to where his mother-in-law stood in the doorway as if she was ready to run back to the car. The look she was giving the boy he held in his arms said she would be taking the child with her when she ran.

At that moment, Zach decided he'd had enough. Enough of trying to be gentle with his in-laws. Enough of letting them dictate when and where he'd see his son while they made him feel inadequate. His son would not spend another moment out of his care. If it meant calling a lawyer and fighting in the courts, so be it. He'd just have to live with the fact that Katherine would never have forgiven him for doing such a thing.

"Kelley, it's so nice to see you again. Come in. We're so glad you could come for the party. I can't wait to meet the rest of Zach's family. Can I get the two of you something to drink?" Lori said from beside him.

Zach could still hear the sound of Lori's voice as she coaxed Kelley into the room as he walked up the stairs to the room he'd made

186　SINGLE DAD'S FAKE FIANCÉE

for his son. Turning on the light, he looked at the crib that had been sitting empty since he'd bought it. Lori had made it up just the night before so Andres would have a place to nap.

"It's a nice room," Butch said from behind him as Zach laid his son on the mattress that had never been used, and then covered Andres with a blanket that Zach couldn't even remember buying.

"I hope he likes it," Zach said, before turning toward his father-in-law. After Katherine had died, Butch had been a rock for Zach, helping him make the funeral plans and listening to Zach when he'd needed someone. He'd always admired the man, had never dreamed that the man he had come to love would fight him over his grandson.

"He will, I'm sure." Butch moved into the room and shut the door behind him. "I hope you don't mind our showing up early. I had to do some talking to convince Kelley to come. It seemed best to just get her in the car before she could come up with any reasons to cancel."

So, his mother-in-law had been giving Butch a hard time about coming. "She was going to cancel? Why?"

Butch rubbed at his face, then stared up at the ceiling. The man had aged more than years since he'd lost his daughter. "We knew what you were doing the moment we got the invitation. I can't say I'm surprised. I've known this day was coming. Expected it."

Butch looked into Zach's eyes, and he understood the pain he saw there. "I don't want to hurt you or Kelley. Katherine wouldn't want me to do that. But I need my son."

Zach glanced down to where Andres slept, with no worries in the world. He had no idea of the war that had been going on around him for the last months.

"I know. I've tried to tell Kelley for months, since you moved, that it was time to let Andres go, but..." Butch ran his hand over his face again. "Katherine's death did something to her. It left a hole."

"And Andres filled it," Zach said. "I know. I saw it from the beginning. I should have done something then. I never should have let Andres go that first day."

"To be honest, I don't know what we would have done if you hadn't. Taking care of Andres helped both of us. It kept us from spending every moment thinking about Katherine." Butch moved toward Zach, his hand coming to rest on Zach's arm. "I know we should have let the two of you go earlier. I know you need

188 SINGLE DAD'S FAKE FIANCÉE

to make your own life. It was selfish of us and I'm sorry for that."

Butch turned to walk away, but Zach stopped him. "So, you're not going to fight me? Because I'm not going to be manipulated into letting him go back to Memphis. He's staying with me."

"I'm not going to fight you. I think Andres will be happy with you and Lori. I like her. She seems to be a nice woman. I also like the way you look at her. It's the first time I've seen your eyes alive except when you're with Andres. I think Katherine would like Lori too. She'd be happy that you've found someone to love."

Zach didn't know what to say, though some of the guilt he felt for the feelings that he was having for Lori eased just a bit.

"I wish I could speak for Kelley, but that woman has always been stubborn. I'll do what I can." Butch gave him a weak smile. "But it will be up to you to convince her that Andres belongs more with you than with us."

Zach waited until Butch left to walk back over to the crib to watch his son sleep. When the boy began to stir, he patted his back as Andres settled back into sleep. "It's okay, son. You're home now. And your daddy is never going to let go of you again."

* * *

Lori looked toward the stairs as Butch came down, disappointed that Zach didn't come down after him. She needed reinforcements.

Keeping Kelley from following her husband up the stairs had almost been more than she could do, but she wanted Zach to have a moment with his son without her taking it over. So she'd taken the woman on a tour through the downstairs with Kelley not saying a word, though every once in a while, Lori would see that mask of disinterest slide away. Even though it was dark, she pointed out the kitchen window to where a fenced-in yard held a play area for Andres. But when she'd seen the paperwork Zach had filled out that morning after one of the nanny interviews he'd done, she'd covered the stack with a cutting board. She wasn't about to start that conversation with Kelley, though she knew from the look on Zach's face as he'd carried his son up the stairs that it would have to happen. There was no way he was letting his son go this time.

"Show me where Andres is sleeping," Kelley said to her husband when he joined them.

"There's no need. Zach's settling him in," Butch told his wife as he walked past the two of them, headed toward the front door. "I'll go get our bags."

Lori tensed. Their bags? They were staying there, with Lori and Zach? Of course they were. Had Lori really thought that Kelley was going to leave Andres here without her?

"Then Lori can show me upstairs where we will be staying," Kelley said, looking at Lori as if the words had been an order.

"Sure. Just give me a moment to get the guest room ready," Lori said, then ran up the stairs as fast as she could, hoping the woman wouldn't follow her.

As she headed down to the guest room, also known as the only other room with a bed besides Zach's room, she stopped at Andres's doorway to find Zach standing over the toddler's crib. Without hesitating, she went to his side and took his arm, hauling him out of the room as she tried not to wake his son. "Did you know they were planning to stay with us?"

"I wasn't expecting them at all tonight, but I'm not surprised they're staying. From what I can tell, it took everything Butch had to get Kelley to agree to come. We had a talk. A good one."

"You can tell me about that later. Right now, we have to figure out what we are going to do before Kelley comes looking for the two of us and finds out that I'm staying in the guest room."

"Why would that be a problem," Zach asked, then moaned. "Because she'd see that the two of us aren't sleeping together which…"

"Which would look really strange for two people engaged and sharing a home," Lori finished for him. "Yeah, because of that. I've got to move my stuff out of the room and into yours. That woman is so high-strung right now, if she sees any evidence that we are not what we say we are, she's going to call us out on it and cause trouble. It's like she's looking for a reason to leave and I have no doubt that she'll try to take Andres with her."

"She's not going to take him. I've already spoken with Butch, but yes, we can talk about that later. What can I do?" Zach asked, his eyes going back to the room where his son slept.

"Just tell them I want to get the room ready and keep them busy for a few minutes," Lori said. Realizing she was still holding on to his arm, she let go. "I'll have to move all my stuff to your room for the night."

As the two of them went in different directions, Lori couldn't ignore the fact that it looked like the two of them might finally be

192 SINGLE DAD'S FAKE FIANCÉE

sharing a bed. She knew that it was entirely inappropriate that she was excited about the prospect. If Zach had wanted her in his bed, he would have asked her. Now it would be like it was being forced on him.

She shoved those thoughts aside as she quickly gathered what belongings she had accumulated after the fire, tossing them into pillowcases. She stripped the bed and made it again with sheets she found in the hall linen closet. After she moved her things to Zach's room, not allowing herself more than one look at the big bed in the center, she headed back down the stairs.

The entryway was empty but she could hear voices...and was that laughter coming from the family room?

Going through the kitchen, she found Kelley with a glass of wine, leaning against the island as Butch and Zach worked on the balloons that had been left to blow up. The two men seemed to be having a good time working together, and for a moment Lori thought she saw a slight smile on Kelley's face.

"It looks like I've missed most of the fun," Lori said as she watched the two men begin to put up the decorations. She nodded when Kelley offered her a glass of wine.

"They've always gotten along so well," Kelley said before taking a drink from her own glass. "Katherine was a daddy's girl. She always said that Zach reminded her of her father with his patience and humor. It made her so happy to see the two of them together."

"She was lucky to have them both," Lori said softly. This softer, vulnerable Kelley was a different part of the woman than Lori normally saw. For the first time she fully understood that Katherine's mother was still deeply grieving over the loss of her daughter. Lori could see now that she'd buried a lot of her grief by putting all of her energy into caring for Andres. No wonder the woman was afraid of losing Andres. With her grandson gone, she'd have no choice but to face that grief.

"Does your father like Zach?" Kelley asked.

The question was so unexpected that Lori had to take a drink of her wine before she answered, making sure to keep her voice steady. "My father left when I was young. I don't know where he is or even if he's still alive."

Kelley turned and looked at her then. "Is that why you're so determined for Zach to have Andres here in Nashville?"

"Maybe that's some of it. But more than that, I'm determined for Zach to have his son be-

194 SINGLE DAD'S FAKE FIANCÉE

cause he deserves him. He loves his son. He'd do anything for him. You know that. You know that Andres belongs with his father."

"He could have been with Andres at our home. There was no reason for him to change things and move to Nashville."

"You had to know that Zach would want to move out with Andres on his own someday. You couldn't expect him to spend the rest of his life living with his in-laws," Lori said.

"I think it's time for bed for this old man," Butch said as he joined them, Zach right behind him. If he'd overheard anything Lori had said, he didn't show it.

"We'll take you up," Zach told them, before taking one of the bags Butch had.

Lori saw that Kelley had taken what looked like a diaper bag, no doubt packed with Andres's things. "We can stop by Andres's room to drop that off."

Lori took the woman to Andres's room, then hustled her out to the guest room where Butch was waiting for her before she could wake the child. It had been a long day and Lori knew the next one could prove to be just as long. She started downstairs to clean up only to meet Zach coming up. She could see that he'd turned off the lights, giving her no reason to go down.

They climbed the stairs together, then stopped at the spot where they normally would have gone separate ways. The night before she had hesitated at that same spot, waiting for Zach to say something, do something, to explain the reason he looked at her with such longing each night, but never said the words she wanted to hear. Couldn't he see the same longing he had for her in her eyes?

But then how could he when she'd never explained to him that she felt that same desire she could see in his eyes? Maybe this was all meant to be. Maybe it was time to speak up and let him know that she wanted him. That while she was faking an engagement with him, there was nothing fake about the need that she had felt from the first night she'd spent there.

She'd talked herself out of knocking on his door last night because she'd been afraid of getting hurt. Tonight, she wasn't going to let her fear stop her.

"I want you," she said, the words inadequate for the desire she felt to be with him. "I want to sleep with you. I want you to hold me tonight. I want to make love with you."

CHAPTER THIRTEEN

Zach sucked in a breath. He'd tried to hide his desire for Lori. She deserved so much better than him. When he'd met her, he'd been so messed up, struggling with his cowardly choice of leaving his son in his in-laws' care after his wife's death. But she'd done something no one else had done. She'd listened to him, then told him to get his act together, make a plan and get his son back. She'd had a belief in him that he hadn't had in himself since Katherine's death. And though he was stronger now, he still didn't deserve someone like Lori, someone with so much love. Love that he didn't know if he would ever be brave enough to return.

But what he did know was that he wanted to hold her, to make love to her, to give her this night that they both wanted.

She looked away from him. Embarrassed for telling him that she wanted him? He lifted her chin till their eyes met. "I want that too. I want you in my bed tonight. I want to make love with you."

He kissed her lips, just a caress at first. She tasted so good as his hands shifted into the soft silkiness of her hair. He tilted her head to take the kiss deeper. Her lips were so soft and pliant as they opened under his demanding mouth. As his tongue danced with hers, his body became hard, his muscles straining as he tried to pull himself back from the temptation of stripping them both bare right there in the hallway. It was only the thought of Kelley and Butch that made him stop the kiss before they could go any further.

He rested his head on hers as he tried to catch his breath. When he raised his eyes to hers, he saw undisguised pleasure there. He smiled at her, then took her hand, leading her down the hall to his room.

When he'd shut the door behind him, he led her to the bed. He moved the two pillowcases filled with clothes off the bed. Not waiting to turn down the bed, he sat and pulled her down to his lap.

"Are we really doing this?" Lori asked as she wrapped her arms around his neck.

"From what I've read in those romance books you recommended, this was inevitable." His lips settled in the curve of her neck and worked their way up as she moved to give him more access, her body pressing into his lap. He stopped for a moment, needing to get a stronger hold on his body's response.

"So, you got to the good parts, huh? Which trope? The fake fiancée or the forced proximity?" Lori asked before she let out a moan as his mouth continued its path up her neck and behind her ear.

"Does it matter?" he asked. He shifted her in his lap as he began to unbutton her blouse. "I can promise you one thing. I won't be faking anything tonight."

"No faking anything tonight, I promise," she swore to him.

He shifted again, letting her feel the hard length of him against her. He felt her body tighten in his arms before she shifted her own body, turning in his arms until she was straddling him. The wicked smile she gave him was all the warning he had before she pressed herself against him and crossed her legs around his back.

His lips took hers, and his hands were trembling as he undid the last button on her blouse and almost ripped it off her body. When he went to undo her bra, her hands came up between them, pushing him away.

"Too slow," she said, undoing her bra and throwing it across the room.

Then her hands began unbuttoning his own shirt before they moved down to the button of his jeans. He almost laughed at the way her eyebrows scrunched into a line and she bit down on her bottom lip as she tried to figure out how to undo his zipper while they sat entwined together.

"Let me help," he said. She gasped as he lifted her up and in one quick twist of their bodies had her lying on her back, his body over hers. He undid the legs she'd crossed around him and stood. He shed his jeans as she wiggled out of her pants, the movement as erotic as any he'd ever seen. Then she slowly peeled her underwear off.

"I thought you said I was going too slow," he said, consumed by a hunger he'd never felt at the sight of her laid out bare on his bed.

The wicked smile on her face made him laugh as he moved over her, then rolled her to her side so that they were facing each other. His hand skimmed down her chest, circling her breast, palming her nipples. His hand swept lower until it slid between her legs. He stopped and her body went still. "I might have learned a little more than how to play a fake fiancé from those romance books."

Then his fingers slid between her folds and entered her. The gasp she made quickly turned into a moan as he continued to stroke her. She pulled his head down to her and kissed him with an intensity that almost undid him as he slipped his fingers in and out, each time sliding between her legs before entering her again. Her body arched against him and his mouth swallowed her moans.

He pulled back and just looked at her. With her hair spread across the bed in tangles, her lips bright red from his kisses and those bright green eyes a little wild, it was a sight he would never forget. She was beautiful in every way, inside and out.

And she deserves better than you.

Yes, yes, she did deserve better than him. She deserved a man with a heart that hadn't been broken. She deserved the type of love you only experience once in a lifetime.

He remembered what Jack had said, that you could feel love again, but would it be enough? Could you love the second time around as deeply as you had loved before?

She reached up for him, running her hands

up his chest to wrap around his neck, pulling him down to her, making him push away all the guilt that wanted to drown him. Her lips touched his and he covered her with his body, the slide of her skin against his own driving him to madness.

No, he wasn't the man that deserved her, they both knew that. But as he entered her, filled her, and felt her quiver as she broke apart in his arms, he swore that for just tonight, he would let himself believe that he could be that man.

Lori stood beside Zach as he introduced his brother and sister-in-law to her and as he held Andres. The pride in his voice as he introduced his son to his family and friends made Lori's heart melt. When they'd woken that morning, she was surprised that there was no awkwardness between the two of them though neither of them commented on the night before. Zach had told her of his conversation with Butch the previous night, and she knew his attention was fixed on having his son with him because that was the most important thing for both of them right then. They still had to worry about how Kelley was going to take the news and how they were going to handle it if she fought

202   SINGLE DAD'S FAKE FIANCÉE

against Butch's decision. But they decided they couldn't let that ruin the party as the rest of the guests had no idea what was going on in the background. And so, they went through the motions of the party.

When Andres, tired from being held by his father, wiggled out of Zach's arms she was surprised when he went to Lori and held up his arms to her. She picked him up and put him on her hips, the weight of him feeling so natural to her. Almost too natural, as she knew she was quickly falling for the toddler just as she had for his father.

The two of them had bonded over bath time that morning after he'd eaten his breakfast. She'd thought it would be a fight when she'd taken the toddler out of his high chair and told Butch and Kelley that she was going to get him ready for the party. But when Kelley had started toward her, Butch had placed an arm in front of her, giving her a look that stopped her. Why Butch was helping her, she didn't know, but she appreciated it. She and Andres had played in the tub till not only was Lori soaked, but the bathroom floor was covered with bubbles. The child's laughter had been so carefree that Lori wondered if he was already feeling at home. But then children accept change so much easier than adults.

She and Zach had already discussed the fact that leaving the only home he knew and not seeing his grandparents every day would be an adjustment for Andres. Zach had decided that asking the nanny he intended to hire to stop by and meet his son might help. Lori just hoped that Kelley didn't run the woman off before he got a chance to give her the job.

No, she wasn't going to let thoughts of what could go wrong ruin this day. Andres was home, and if Butch was to be believed, he'd be staying there with them. No, not with them, with Zach. Her part in this was just temporary and she needed to remember that.

Last night, after they'd made love, there had been no words of love or of a future together. So wouldn't that mean that last night had really just been sex, not making love? But that wasn't what it had felt like to her. She'd started to tell Zach how she felt afterward. How she'd been falling in love with him since that night at the wedding. But she held back. He'd made it clear that he didn't want to be romantically involved with anyone from the beginning. Telling him that she loved him now would put their friendship at risk. Last night she'd felt like one of her romance novel heroines, except she knew she wasn't going to get a happily-ever-after. They'd had a wonderful night together, but nothing had changed between the two of them. She was there for a purpose, and if things went right today, Zach wouldn't need her after tonight. But was it too much to ask for just a little more time with him before she left? The longer she stayed the harder it was going to be for her to leave. And she had to start making plans for her and Baby Janiah. But still...

A few weeks ago, she would have sworn that all she needed to make her happy was to be a mother. Now she knew that wasn't true. She needed more. She needed a man to love her and one she could love without having to hide her feelings. But it wasn't just any man she wanted. She wanted Zach. She wanted him to be that man. Only, he couldn't be. Not by any fault of his own, it was just the way it was. He'd lost someone he loved and he didn't want to risk loving someone again, if he even could love someone again.

"Can he go outside with us?" One of Zach's nieces, Helene, asked from beside her. Though the girl looked to be barely twelve, Lori had seen how she mothered her little brother and sister.

"I don't see why not," Lori said, looking to where Zach had stood just moments earlier, but found that he'd walked off without her noticing. "Go ahead outside. Just let me check with his dad and then I'll bring him out."

She walked through the house, still carrying Andres while speaking with Zach's family and then Kelley and Butch, but no one seemed to know where Zach had gone. She was about to head up the stairs when he walked in from the front porch holding his phone in his hand. When his eyes met hers, she knew something was wrong. Just moments earlier he'd been laughing and joking, now he looked as if the weight of the world had been handed to him.

Her heart seemed to stutter with the only word she could get out, "Janiah?"

"That was Dr. Davis. She's got weekend call, but I asked her to keep me up-to-date on Baby Girl Doe." The fact that he was using the proper name for Janiah sounded so cold that it sent a chill through Lori's body.

"What happened?" she asked, her arms tightening around the little boy squirming in her arms.

"She's had another seizure, this one lasted longer than the first one. They've titrated the morphine and they're taking her for an MRI now."

"Okay, so this happens sometimes, right? You've had patients in the NICU for a month for withdrawals. It's just going to take some time."

"Dr. Davis and I are concerned about the new seizure. Neither one of us would have expected another one at this point. But the real concern is—" he held out his arms to his son, taking Andres from her, then put his arm around her waist "—she hasn't woken up since the seizure. She's only minimally responsive right now."

Lori's mind raced through all the reasons for Janiah being unresponsive and went straight to the worst-case scenario. "Do you think she has a bleed?"

"It could be that she's just postictal. She could wake up and be fine. We'll just have to wait and see."

But Lori didn't want to wait, she wanted to see Janiah for herself. "I have to go. She shouldn't be alone, not now. I'm sorry, I know it's your birthday, but I need to be with her. She needs to know someone loves her."

"It's okay, I've already told Dr. Davis you would be coming. I'd go too, but..." Zach looked to where his guests were gathered and Lori saw that Kelley was headed toward them.

"What's going on?" Kelley asked, reaching out for her grandson. When her grandson shied away from her, turning into his daddy's shoulder, the woman looked like someone had slapped her.

"Kelley, why don't you take Andres out to play with his cousins, if that's okay with you Zach?" Lori asked. While she thought the woman was overbearing and had definitely been wrong in her treatment of her son-in-law, Kelley loved her grandson. "Helene was asking to take him out there with them."

Turning to Zach she said, "I don't know how long I'll be gone. Can you tell everyone goodbye for me?"

"You're going somewhere? You're going to leave the party?" Kelley called as Lori headed up the stairs.

Lori ignored her. Zach could explain for her. Right now, she needed to get to the hospital because there was a baby, one she had begun to think of as her own, surrounded by doctors and nurses, but still all alone. Someone had to look out for her, and Lori had chosen from the moment that little newborn had clutched her finger to be the one to do it.

208 SINGLE DAD'S FAKE FIANCÉE

* * *

Zach shut the door behind Lori. He didn't like the idea of her going to the hospital alone. She needed someone with her if the news they got back from the CT turned out to be bad. She had been so determined to be there for Janiah, but who would be there for Lori? Somehow, he knew in his heart that he should be the one there with Lori. Not as a doctor, but as Lori's friend? Lover? What?

He'd sworn to himself that he would not get involved with another woman, not romantically. But wasn't it about time he accepted the changes Lori had brought into his life? Not Andres, though she'd certainly given him the courage and support for him to get his son, but the other changes in his life. He was happy. For the first time since he'd lost his wife, he was healing. He felt like he might actually be able to love again.

And it scared him. Scared him so bad that this morning when he'd gotten up, he'd acted like nothing had happened between the two of them last night. While all the time he'd been thrilled to see Lori lying next to him. For several minutes, he'd just lain there and let the fact that she was there beside him sink in. He'd expected it to feel awkward, but instead it had felt right. It had felt like a part of him had healed. The pain of losing Katherine would never go away, he knew that. But he remembered what Jack had told him too. There was room in his heart to love again, if he was willing to allow it.

But still there was that fear of going through the pain of loss again. He wasn't sure he'd be strong enough to survive another loss. He'd failed Andres before, he couldn't risk doing that again.

The doorbell rang and he looked at his watch. Carol, the new nanny, was right on time. Before he even opened the door, a plan started forming in his mind.

After he explained about the party, he took Carol to the most important person she needed to meet. While Andres was shy at first, it didn't take the woman but a few moments to get him to warm up to her. He'd known the moment he'd met her that she would be perfect for dealing with both Andres and Kelley with her Mary Poppins looks and her sweet but firm manner.

"Is there any chance you're free to start this afternoon? I have someone at the hospital I need to go see, but I don't want to leave Andres." He'd only just offered the woman the job but he had to ask. The longer Lori was at the hospital by herself, the worse he felt. He knew her mother was working because she'd been unable to attend the party. If Carol couldn't do it, his other choice would be Kelley and Butch, something that his mother-in-law would be sure to use against him.

"I'm free and happy to work, though I'd like to be walked through the rest of the house if you've got the time. I like to know the layout before I take a job. Little ones can escape into all kinds of places. It's better to know where dangers might lie," Carol said.

"No problem. I appreciate the help. I just need to introduce you to Andres's grandparents first," Zach said as he took her upstairs. When they made it back downstairs, he took her through the kitchen to the family room where most of the guests, including his in-laws, had gathered. Then he took her up to the second most important person she needed to meet.

The introductions were awkward as the two women seemed to be sizing each other up. Butch, the smart one, managed to escape into another room. Zach was left unarmed as Kelley began shooting questions at Carol faster than she could answer them.

"The agency runs a background check and I've checked Carol's references. They've all been glowing. She's more than qualified to care for Andres." Zach turned from Kelley to Carol. "I really appreciate you stepping in and helping me. I'll be back as soon as possible."

"What? You're leaving too?" Kelley asked. "I don't understand. You're supposed to be off. You never did explain why Lori had to go see this Baby Jane. And now you're going too? You have guests."

"Who are all welcome to stay or leave. I've spoken with my brother who will be happy to stay until the guests leave and Carol will be here with Andres, so if you and Butch need to head home I understand."

"I'm not leaving my grandson with a stranger. This is exactly what I've been telling you. You are not prepared to care for a child. I'm going to talk to Butch right now and I can promise you that we will be here when you get back."

He was tired of all this arguing and he was tired of trying to placate his in-laws. He'd not heard a word from Lori or Dr. Davis. He needed to leave. He needed to see the baby and Lori. "Fine. Stay. We'll talk when I get back. Until then, Carol will be staying as Andres's nanny. I expect you to be polite."

Before Kelley could say another word, he walked out the door, leaving his mother-in-law speechless for the first time since he'd met her.

CHAPTER FOURTEEN

LORI SAT AND watched a tech apply electrodes to Janiah's little scalp. She wanted to hold the newborn and reassure her that she wasn't alone, that there was someone there to watch over her, but all Lori could do was watch and wait. And it left her feeling useless.

She'd arrived at the hospital to find that Janiah had had another seizure, this one lasting longer than the other one. She'd spoken to the neurologist that had been consulted, but all she had been able to do was suggest a medication change. When the neurologist had asked what her relationship to the baby was, Lori had been at a loss for words. Not knowing what to say, Lori had been honest and told the woman about the mother's abandonment and her request for fostering the baby. Because Lori had delivered the baby, she knew it did give her access to the baby's medical care, but it did not give her any right as far as making decisions.

So, after speaking with the nurse, she called Jessica, the case manager, and notified her of Janiah's health care concerns. After that all she could do was sit and watch as nurses, doctors and techs cared for the child she'd come to think of as her own.

So she just sat and worried about Janiah, about the baby's future and about their future together. And when she wasn't worrying about the baby, she worried about her and Zach. What would happen between the two of them now? Would they remain friends? Lovers?

No, not lovers. She knew that wouldn't work. Not for her. So, friends. Good friends. But would that be enough after what they'd shared, not only last night, but the last three weeks. She'd never been so close to anyone. Never felt so comfortable around someone. Not like the way she felt around Zach.

Someone moved next to her and she looked up and there he was standing beside her. Zach. As if her heart had willed him to come to her. At the sight of those brown eyes of his, her heart sang with a joy it had no right to. Then she realized what his being there could mean. Did the pediatrician and neurosurgeon not want to tell her how serious Janiah's condition was? "They called you? Is it bad news?"

214   SINGLE DAD'S FAKE FIANCÉE

"No, I came for you and Baby Janiah," Zach said, pulling up a chair beside her.

"But what about the party? Kelley? You know she'll use this against you," she said. "Butch might understand that Andres belongs with you, but I don't think Kelley is ready to let go. She still seems to think that you are going to move back to Memphis and live with them as just one big happy family."

"She can't really believe that. And I asked the nanny I hired, Carol, to stay with Andres for a few hours. It will give Kelley a chance to see that single parents with demanding jobs like ours can make sure our children are cared for even if we can't always be there. Besides, it doesn't matter what she thinks anymore. I've tried to be respectful to Kelley and Butch for Katherine and also Andres's sakes, but I've had enough. Butch understands that. Hopefully he can make his wife understand that too before I return tonight."

An alarm went off on one of the monitors and Lori jumped up. Zach's arm came up and around her, and as she lost her balance, he pulled her to his side. "Be careful. It's okay. Her heart rate is just a little high right now. Probably from all the attention she's been getting. I take it they got the MRI?"

"Yes, but I haven't heard anything as far as the results. I thought maybe Dr. Davis had called you and that was why you were here." Lori stepped away from Zach, the warmth of him making her want to curl into his arms, something that she couldn't let herself do. She had to be strong. She wouldn't always have him there to lean on.

"No, I haven't heard anything from them since the first call. I'm sure they'll tell you what they've found as soon as possible."

"Will they?" Lori asked. "I've been here watching everyone working so hard to help her, and all I can do is sit here. And the only reason I've been given that privilege is because I was the midwife that delivered her."

Zach looked at her with surprise. "You've been by this baby's side since that day, making sure she has someone to look out for her when her own mother left her within an hour of her birth. Everyone in this nursery knows that. Yes, they have to be careful because of the privacy laws and yes, they've been able to keep you informed because you are involved as a midwife with her delivery. But does that make a difference? We all know it's more than the job with you and Janiah. And from what

SINGLE DAD'S FAKE FIANCÉE

the staff says about the way she responds to you, she knows it too."

Lori walked over to where Janiah lay, her head now bandaged with gauze over all the electrodes attached to her tiny head. There was an IV in each arm, one which was attached to a bag of lactated ringers to keep her hydrated, the other Lori had seen them using for the IV morphine and other medications. They'd also placed a tube in the baby's nose that went to her stomach so they could feed her. How did all those mothers who knew nothing about the medical world stand seeing their babies this way? Lori knew the necessity of every one of these tubes, but they still had the ability to scare her. The sight of an innocent baby being surrounded by all of those tubes and beeping monitors was just too much. All she wanted at that moment was to hold Janiah tight and reassure her that she wasn't alone and she was going to be okay.

Zach's hand came to rest on her shoulder, and that was when she realized that he was there for her for the same reason she was there for Janiah. He didn't want her to feel that she was all alone either.

But she would be. Soon, if things went as she hoped with her application for fostering

Janiah, she'd be a single mother. Zach would be there as a friend, she hoped, but he would be busy with the life he'd planned. The one he wanted with just him and his son. She wouldn't have him to lean on then. Oh, she'd still have her friends and her mother, but she would still be alone at night when she put Janiah to bed.

After talking to Zach at the wedding she'd realized that she had only been shopping for a baby's daddy, instead of looking for someone to love, because she'd thought having a child in her life was all she had ever really wanted. It wasn't like a child would leave her, abandon her. A man though? How could she ever hope to trust one with her heart when she knew they could just up and leave her at any time? How could she live with that fear?

But now? After living with Zach and playing at being his fiancée, she knew she wanted more. She wanted that forever love, the kind of love that he had been up-front about not ever wanting again. And for the first time, she understood how he felt. Because she didn't want just any love, she wanted Zach's love. She wanted to be able to trust him with her love. She wanted him to love her the same way that she loved him.

And if he wasn't ever able to give her that

love? Was it possible that she would become like him? Was it possible that she'd never be able to let go of her love for him and find someone else to love her? Would she always wander around in her crowd of friends, but still be all alone?

The monitors above Janiah's head went off again, the sounds echoing through the nursery as she watched Janiah's body stiffen, and her eyelids begin to blink rapidly. She was having another seizure. Lori moved away as Zach stepped over to the isolette where Janiah continued to seize.

Four hours later, Lori and Zach dragged themselves back to Zach's house. The news from the MRI hadn't been good. While she'd been hoping that it was just the drug withdrawal that was causing Janiah's seizures, it had been determined that it was something worse. The neurologist and doctor had both come to the conclusion after reviewing the results of the MRI that Janiah was suffering from neonatal encephalopathy due to what looked like a small brain injury making her neurologically unstable. While the brain injury appeared so small that it hadn't been seen on the CT, they suspected that it had been present at birth and probably stemmed from a hypoxic injury during labor.

And while Lori didn't want to believe it, she couldn't deny the fact that the baby could have been in fetal distress for hours while her mother had been in labor. There was no fetal tracing to review. The mother had been placed on the monitor just moments before giving birth. How long Janiah could have been in distress causing her to become hypoxic, they had no way of knowing. All they could do now was hope that the damage was mild, something that the neurologist had assured her was possible. It had all been too much to take in at one time. For now, the seizures had stopped and Janiah was stable.

Her plan had been to shower and then take a short nap before returning to the hospital, but when Zach opened the door, she knew that wasn't going to happen anytime soon. Standing at the door was Kelley who must have been watching out the window waiting for their return. Zach had told her that he'd received several texts and a call from his mother-in-law while they were at the hospital, but he'd ignored them once he'd made sure that Andres was okay.

But now there was nothing to do but face

220   SINGLE DAD'S FAKE FIANCÉE

the woman, something Lori had neither the time nor the patience for. She started to walk past Kelley until she saw that there was another woman standing behind her. Was this the nanny Zach had hired? If it was, it would be a miracle if she didn't quit after being left all afternoon with Kelley.

"Would you please tell this woman that she can leave? The woman has refused to leave us alone with our grandson." Kelley's face was turning red, telling them all just how angry she was at not getting her way with the nanny.

"Lori this is Carol, Andres's new nanny. Carol, this is Lori," Zach said, introducing the woman as she stepped around Kelley.

"It's nice to meet you," she said before turning to Zach. "I'm so sorry if I misunderstood your instructions."

"There was no misunderstanding. I appreciate you helping me out today. Let me walk you out to your car," Zach said, before looking at Lori. "I'll be right back."

Lori watched the two of them walk out the door, then glanced back at the stairs wishing for a way to escape. She realized Butch had come into the room at some point. The man looked as if he'd had a day almost as bad as hers. Leaving him now to deal with his wife alone didn't seem like the right thing to do.

"Why don't we all go have a glass of wine?" Lori asked. "Then we can talk about everything like rational adults."

Lori knew she'd used the wrong words the moment they'd come out. She was tired and irritable and not in the right frame of mind to deal with the woman.

"Are you saying I'm not rational? Is that why Zach felt the need to ask the nanny to stay with Andres? Because what, I've suddenly become what? Unstable?"

Lori felt a whole new respect for the poor nanny who'd had to deal with this while they'd been at the hospital. "I didn't mean to imply that you were not being rational. I was referring to all of us. We need to sit down and talk about how things are changing."

"I don't see why things need to change at all. There's no reason for my grandson to have a nanny, an outsider, when Butch and I can be with him all the time. Zach can move back to Memphis and things can be like they use to be. We'll be there to make sure that nothing happens to Andres when Zach's not there."

Kelley was becoming frantic now and Lori knew she needed to deescalate the situation,

222 SINGLE DAD'S FAKE FIANCÉE

but her patience had been strained all day waiting for doctors and medical results. Besides, hadn't Zach been patient for months? What had that gotten him? Nothing but more of the same. Excuses as to why his son needed to stay with his grandparents. It was more than Lori could take. "Keeping Andres to yourself isn't what he needs. You won't always be able to keep him safe, no matter how hard you try. He needs to experience the world, not be wrapped up in cotton and hidden away."

"That's not..." Kelley began, before Lori interrupted her.

"Yes, it is. That's exactly what you are doing. You've even tried to hide him away from his father. His father who loves him so much that he is willing to do anything to have his son with him."

"I don't care if you are going to marry Zach, you can't talk to me that way. You don't understand."

Lori tried to make herself take a breath and calm down. She understood that Kelley was just panicking because she knew that she had already lost where Andres was concerned. But there was a baby with no one except for her in the NICU right now. While here they were arguing over a little boy who was so lucky to

DEANNE ANDERS 223

have so many people love him that they were ready to fight for him. Life wasn't fair. Lori had learned that early in life. But this...this was unnecessary and it needed to end now.

"No, it's you that doesn't understand. Zach has done everything you've asked of him for months. Yet it takes me, someone who's only known him for a short time to see how he's being manipulated by you. You've used his lack of judgment when his mind was crowded with grief against him for months. I understand that you were grieving too. And Zach saw that. He gave in to you so many times because he knew you were grieving like him. But then, when you could see that he was ready to raise his son, you wouldn't give him back."

"We..." Kelley started but stopped when Butch put his hand on her shoulder.

"Do you even realize how far Zach was willing to go when you threatened to take him to court? He was willing to do anything, even marry someone he barely knew. This engagement of ours, it's all been to help him get his son back. You were so set on the fact that he couldn't raise Andres alone that he was willing to fake an engagement to me to make you think that he had found someone to love and help him raise his son. But this wasn't even

224 SINGLE DAD'S FAKE FIANCÉE

about you thinking he wasn't capable. It was just another excuse you were using to hold on to Andres. To use the boy to fill the hole in your heart that losing your daughter left, wasn't it?"

Kelley had stopped interrupting her and it wasn't until she noticed that Butch was looking past her that she realized Zach had come up behind her.

"You lied to us?" Butch asked. "I trusted you, thought that you were moving ahead with your life, as Katherine would have wanted you to, but you were lying to us the whole time."

It was the disappointment on the man's face that finally cut through the anger that had spurred Lori's rant to Kelley. Now, realizing what she had said, what she had done, Lori knew she'd gone too far. She'd just ruined everything for Zach.

She heard Zach answer as he tried to explain things, but she couldn't stay and listen to Kelley and Butch berating him. If she'd just ignored Kelley and gone upstairs to begin with, this wouldn't have happened. She headed up the stairs not looking back. When she got to the top of the stairs she went to Andres's room, checking to see if the voices that she could still hear had awakened him.

But the child lay still sleeping in his crib. Would he ever know how hard each of those adults had fought for him? Would he realize how lucky he was to have a father that would do anything to be in his life every day? Covering him with a small blanket, she left him to his dreams. Maybe someday, when he was much older, Zach would tell him about Lori and how she'd tried to help him.

She left the baby sleeping soundly and headed to Zach's room. Opening the door, the first thing she saw was the bed they'd shared the night before. Was it only just a few hours ago that Zach had held her in his arms? It seemed as if it was a lifetime ago that they'd lain there together, their bodies joined together so perfectly. She'd wanted one more night in Zach's bed, just one more. She'd promised herself that one more night would be enough. She'd lied. But then hadn't she been lying for weeks now? She truly had to be the worst fake fiancée that there had ever been. Even the ones in her romance books had done a better job than she had.

She'd fallen for a man who had made it more than clear that he didn't want to ever love another woman. She'd slept with the man, know-

226　SINGLE DAD'S FAKE FIANCÉE

ing it was just going to make things more complicated between them. And then she'd messed up and lost her temper, telling the last people she needed to tell that it had all been a ruse.

All she could do now was leave before she messed things up anymore. Glancing around the room, she grabbed the pillowcases which held the small amount of stuff she owned and went into the bathroom to get the rest. She came out and allowed herself one more look around the room before she shut the door on all the hopes and dreams she'd allowed herself the night before.

She was glad to see that there was no one waiting for her when she started down the stairs. But when she got to the bottom step, she could hear voices coming from the kitchen. Zach's voice, but not the one he usually used around his in-laws, the gentle voice that was patient with the older couple out of love and respect. No, this time his voice was hard as steel. He was fighting back, at last. A part of Lori relaxed. It told her that there was no way his in-laws would be taking Andres from him tonight.

She slipped out the door without looking back, assured from what she'd heard that even though she'd made a mess of things, Zach would get the one thing he wanted in life. His son.

CHAPTER FIFTEEN

IT HAD TAKEN over an hour for Kelley to calm down enough for Butch to get her in the car to make their trip back to Memphis. Zach had offered for the two of them to stay another night, but Butch had insisted it would be easier now that the decision had been made to keep some distance from Andres for a while. Zach had quickly agreed. As soon as their taillights had disappeared, he'd rushed up to Andres's room to make sure it wasn't a dream. Finding his son asleep in his room, the next thing he'd done was to look for Lori so he could tell her the good news. Andres was totally his now.

He'd expected to find her asleep in his bed. When she wasn't there, he'd called the nursery to make sure she'd made it there safely. Once he'd spoken to one of the NICU nurses who confirmed that she was there, he'd relaxed. Only to find moments later that he was actually angry at her. Not for telling Kelley and

Butch about the fact that they had been faking a relationship—his mother-in-law was good at getting people to lose their temper and say things they wished they hadn't said. No, that wasn't why he was angry. He was angry that she'd taken all her things with her, leaving him with no doubts of her not returning, without even talking to him. It looked like she had decided that since there was no more reason to pretend to be his fiancée, she could just leave and forget about him. What about last night? What about the weeks they'd shared together? Was he supposed to pretend now that the time they'd spent together had never happened? Was that what she wanted?

Wasn't that what you told her you wanted?

Yes. Yes, that was what he'd told her he wanted. No romantic entanglements. No talk of love or a happily-ever-after. Just friendship. But friendship would never have included the two of them sharing a bed. Nor would it make him feel this ache in his chest.

He saw the romance book lying on his nightstand where he'd been reading it a few nights earlier. It was the first one he'd picked up. He'd made it to the last two chapters of the book. So far, the couple had managed to fool everyone with their fake engagement, but they had begun

230 SINGLE DAD'S FAKE FIANCÉE

to have feelings for each other, making things more complicated between the two of them.

Sitting down, he turned to the last page he'd read. Maybe with the help of these two characters, he'd be able to figure out things between the two of them.

Zach saw her the moment he walked into the nursery. He'd known she'd be there. According to the NICU nurses, she'd been there every night for the last three days, coming and going between office hours and then spending hours at a time by Janiah's bedside each night. He'd gotten another doctor to cover for him so that he could get Andres settled.

And he'd thought about Lori.

"How is she this evening?" he asked, though he'd kept up with the baby's condition through the nurses.

Lori looked up at him, her eyes underlined by dark shadows. She was wearing herself out fast. She needed rest. She needed someone to care for her like she cared for Janiah. "She hasn't had a seizure since…since the night of the party, so the neurologist is hopeful. She's begun eating again. I just finished feeding her. The nurses say she eats better for me than for them so I try to help out."

"They told me. They also tell me that you're wearing yourself down. You need to take care of yourself so that when she gets discharged from the hospital, you'll be ready."

"I know," she said, looking back to where the baby lay sleeping. "How's Andres?"

"He's getting used to all the changes. We both are, I guess."

"I'm sorry for what happened with Kelley and Butch. I never meant for that to happen. I just…"

"It worked out for the best. I had a hard talk with them. I don't think that they intended for things to turn out the way they did when they first offered to help out with Andres. I think they really wanted to help me. They seem to realize now that it was time to let go. I think seeing me move on helped them, even if it wasn't all real."

"I'm glad for you and Andres. The two of you belong together," Lori said, her words ringing true.

"Do you have time for a walk? We could go up to the garden," he said. He held a hand out to her and waited. When she took his hand, he let the breath he'd been holding go. He led her to the one set of elevators that would take them

232 SINGLE DAD'S FAKE FIANCÉE

to the rooftop garden. At this time of night, he knew they should find it deserted.

"I guess we should talk. I haven't said anything to anyone about ending the engagement. I wanted to talk to you first," Lori said as the elevator doors closed. "And I need to give you this back."

She took the diamond ring he'd bought her off her finger and handed it to him. Unsure what to do with it, he stuck it in his pocket.

He was more nervous than he had ever been. He didn't have the words to explain his feeling like the hero in the romance books he'd read. He just knew that in the last three days not having Lori in his life had been miserable. He'd realized then that it didn't matter how scared he was of loving someone again, of losing someone again. Not having Lori at all would be just as painful.

The doors opened to the garden and they stepped out. There were lights strung across the paths that wandered in and out of the raised flower beds that the hospital volunteers took care of.

He tried to think of something that a romantic hero would say, but nothing came. He decided it was best to admit the truth. "I miss you."

"It was best that I left when I did. After what happened that night... I guess I started to believe in our pretense myself." Lori stopped walking and he stopped beside her. "I've read too many romances. I should know by now that real life doesn't work that way."

Unable to stop himself, he took her hand. "That night was wonderful, but it wasn't enough. You're right, real life isn't like the books. But that night was real, just like all the other nights we've spent together were real. This...how I feel about you...it's real. That's what I want—a real relationship. Not one built on pretense. I want you with me because you want to be with me. I don't care if you're my real girlfriend, or my real fiancée. Because this love I feel for you isn't a pretend love, it's real."

"I don't understand. I thought you said you couldn't ever love someone again." Lori pulled away from him, stepped back. "How do you know that it's real? How do I know you haven't gotten carried away with the pretense like I did?"

"Do you really believe that's what happened? If so, wouldn't it all have ended when you told Kelley the truth? When you ended the pretense?" He stepped up to her. He had to let her know how much he loved her. But how?

234 SINGLE DAD'S FAKE FIANCÉE

"I once believed that I would never be able to love another person in my lifetime. Not only because of my fear of having to feel that loss, but because I didn't think I had any more love to give. But I was wrong. You opened up a part of my heart that I didn't know existed. Now all I need is for you to walk in and take it."

He took her face in his hands. "Now tell me the truth. No pretense. No lies. Do you love me, Lori?"

His heart raced as he waited for her answer. What if she really had been caught up in the pretense?

Her hands came up and covered his. Her tired eyes were suddenly bright with tears and her lips seemed to tremble as she said, "Oh, yes, Zach. I really, really do love you."

EPILOGUE

THERE WERE NO pink roses in crystal vases. There was no string quartet. Instead, Lori and Zach had decided that a child-friendly ceremony and reception fit the two of them better as they wouldn't consider getting married without Andres and Janiah at their side. So, it had been decided that the wedding would be held outside. They'd found the perfect venue with a garden path that led to a large courtyard and plenty of room for the kids to run and play.

It had been just over a year since the night they'd attend Sky and Jared's wedding. Sky liked to take credit for the two of them finding each other, while Bree and Knox claimed that they had witnessed the moment they'd fallen in love. All four friends knew that Lori and Zach's first engagement hadn't been real, but they all seemed to want to ignore it. Lori choose to let them.

236   SINGLE DAD'S FAKE FIANCÉE

"It's almost time. Are you ready?" her mother asked.

Lori looked down at the vintage tea-length dress that she'd somehow managed to keep clean while chasing Janiah around the dressing room, trying to get the bow in the toddler's hair. They'd both been laughing and out of breath by the time Lori had caught her. Looking over at her daughter now, she could see the bow was tilted to one side, but she didn't care. The fact that her daughter was healthy and able to run and play was a miracle that she celebrated every day. There were still obstacles ahead of them, her growth rate was behind and there were developmental delays, but Lori knew that together she and Zach would face those as they came.

She held her hand out to Janiah. "Let's go see your daddy."

Then taking her mom's hand, she started down the stone pathway where her friends and family waited.

The first faces she saw when they turned the corner that took them into the courtyard were those of Sky and Jared. And in their arms, was Baby Jack, named after his grandfather who sat beside him. Lori had delivered the baby just a month ago. Handing that baby to her friend had been a dream come true for both of them.

Beside Sky, Bree and Knox sat with their daughter, Ally, who had excitedly informed Lori the night before that she was going to be a big sister in six months. Though Bree had already told her, Lori acted surprised for the little girl's sake.

Lori spotted Kelley and Butch in the next aisle, the two of them waving at their grandson who stood at the front. Lori couldn't say that things had all gone smoothly between Zach and his in-laws, but they were working on it. It didn't hurt that Butch and Kelley had been given unlimited time with Andres. It had become a habit for the two of them to visit every other weekend which Lori thought was just as good for Andres as it was for his grandparents.

They stopped and her mother kissed her cheek before taking Janiah and sitting beside Jack.

As soon as her mother and daughter were settled, Lori allowed herself to look to the front of the courtyard where Zach stood holding their son's hand. In a matching dark suit, the two-and-a-half-year-old was almost as handsome as his father.

Unable to help herself, she waved at her lit-

238 SINGLE DAD'S FAKE FIANCÉE

tle boy, only realizing her mistake when Andres pulled away from Zach and ran down the aisle to meet her. Laughing, she gave her son a hug before taking his hand in hers. Then she looked up to see that Zach had followed his son down the aisle.

"Ready to do this?" he asked her, his smile wide and his brown eyes filled with love.

Lori looked from Zach to their son, then smiled back at him. "Hold on one moment."

Hurrying back to her mother, Lori took Janiah into her arms and then walked back to where Zach and Andres waited.

"Ready now?" Zach asked, taking his daughter from Lori.

"Yes, now we're all ready."

* * * * *

*If you missed the previous story in the
Nashville Midwives trilogy,
then check out*
The Rebel Doctor's Secret Child

*And if you enjoyed this story,
check out these other great reads from
Deanne Anders*

Unbuttoning the Bachelor Doc
A Surgeon's Christmas Baby
Flight Nurse's Florida Fairy Tale

All available now!

Reader Service

Enjoyed your book?

Try the perfect subscription for Romance readers and get more great books like this delivered right to your door.

See why over 10+ million readers have tried Harlequin Reader Service.

Start with a Free Welcome Collection with free books and a gift—valued over $20.

Choose any series in print or ebook.
See website for details and order today:

TryReaderService.com/subscriptions